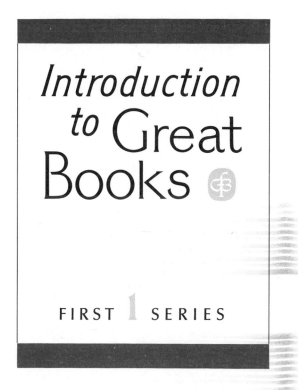

Introduction *to* Great Books

FIRST 1 SERIES

The Great Books Foundation

A nonprofit educational corporation

First Printing

98765432

Published and distributed by

The Great Books Foundation
A Nonprofit Educational Corporation
35 East Wacker Drive, Suite 2300
Chicago, Illinois 60601-2298

Formerly published as Junior Great Books Series Ten

Acknowledgments

All possible care has been taken to trace ownership and secure permission for each selection in this series. The Great Books Foundation wishes to thank the following authors, publishers, and representatives for permission to reprint copyright material:

Why War? from THE COLLECTED PAPERS OF SIGMUND FREUD, edited by Ernest Jones, M.D. Copyright © 1959 by Basic Books, Publishers, Inc., by arrangement with the Hogarth Press, Ltd. and The Institute of Psycho-Analysis, London. By permission of the publisher. Lines from "In Memory of Sigmund Freud" from *W. H. Auden: Collected Poems*, edited by Edward Mendelson. Copyright © 1940, 1964 by W. H. Auden. Reprinted by permission of Random House, Inc.

The Melian Dialogue from THUCYDIDES: THE HISTORY OF THE PELOPONNESIAN WAR, edited in translation by Sir R. W. Livingstone (1943). Reprinted by permission of Oxford University Press.

The Social Me from PSYCHOLOGY: BRIEFER COURSE by William James. Copyright © 1962 by The Crowell-Collier Publishing Co. By permission of Macmillan Publishing Co., Inc.

Rothschild's Fiddle from THE OXFORD CHEKHOV, Volume VII, Stories 1893-1895, translated and edited by Ronald Hingley. Copyright © 1978 by Ronald Hingley. Reprinted by permission of Oxford University Press.

Chelkash, translated by Margaret Wettlin, from FROM KARAMZIN TO BUNIN, AN ANTHOLOGY OF RUSSIAN SHORT STORIES, edited by Carl R. Proffer. Copyright © 1969 by Indiana University Press. By permission of Indiana University Press.

How an Aristocracy May Be Created by Industry from DEMOCRACY IN AMERICA by Alexis de Tocqueville, edited by J. P. Mayer and Max Lerner, a new translation by George Lawrence. Copyright © 1966 in the English translation by Harper & Row, Publishers, Inc. Reprinted by permission of the publisher.

Observation and Experiment from AN INTRODUCTION TO THE STUDY OF EXPERIMENTAL MEDICINE by Claude Bernard, translated by Henry Copley Greene. Published by Macmillan & Co., Ltd., 1927. Reprinted by permission of Dover Publications, Inc.

Everything That Rises Must Converge from EVERYTHING THAT RISES MUST CONVERGE by Flannery O'Connor. Copyright © 1961, 1965 by The Estate of Mary Flannery O'Connor. Reprinted by permission of Farrar, Straus & Giroux, Inc.

An Essay in Aesthetics from VISION AND DESIGN by Roger Fry. Reprinted by permission of the Literary Estate of Roger Fry and Chatto & Windus Ltd.

On Studying from SOME LESSONS IN METAPHYSICS by José Ortega y Gasset, translated by Mildred Adams. Copyright © 1969 by W. W. Norton & Company, Inc. By permission of W. W. Norton & Company, Inc.

Contents

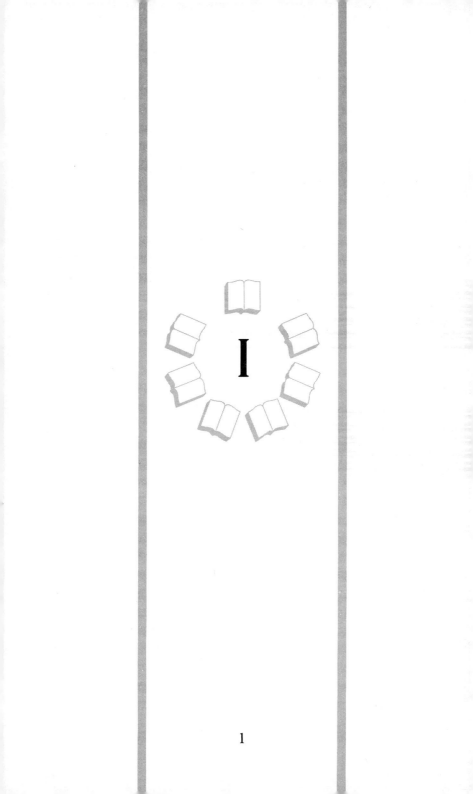

I

Shared Inquiry

A Great Books discussion explores the meaning of a selection that everyone in the group has read in advance. Discussion begins with a leader's interpretive question—a question about a problem of meaning that interests her in the selection. After reading the selection carefully, she has no answer to her question or she thinks that her question can be answered in more than one way. In either case, she wants to explore it with the group. Because leaders and group members work together to try to resolve such problems of meaning, we call the method of discussion *shared inquiry.*

As you discuss the problem, the leader will ask questions for several purposes: to help you clarify your remarks or support your answers with evidence from the selection, to make sure everyone will be given a chance to offer opinions, and to keep discussion moving toward a resolution of the problem.

As a group member, you need not wait to be called on. You may speak up at any time. You may respond directly to other group members as well as to the leader. You may express agreement or disagreement with what others say, add your own thoughts, or ask questions related to the problem being discussed. If you are called on but have nothing to say at the moment, you are equally free not to answer. If you have an idea that you are unsure of, or if you don't know whether your idea is a good one, don't be afraid to express it anyway—it may prove more valuable than you think.

To encourage group members to think for themselves and to guarantee that no one is excluded from discussion, shared inquiry has four rules:

1. **No one may take part in the discussion without first reading the selection.** If you have not read the selection, you cannot contribute to the discussion because you are unprepared to offer opinions and to support them with evidence from the selection.

2. **Discuss only the selection that everyone has read.** If you refer to other essays or stories, the participants who have not read them will be denied a chance to contribute to the discussion. This rule also enables the group to check the validity of what is said by referring to the assigned selection.

3. **Do not introduce outside opinions unless you can back them up with evidence from the selection.** If you get an idea about the meaning of a selection from an outside source—for example, the opinion of someone you know or an insight from another book—you may use the idea in discussion only if you can express it in your own words and support it with evidence from the selection.

4. **Leaders may only ask questions—they may not answer them.** If leaders stated their own opinions about the meaning of a selection, you might feel less inclined to think for yourself. You might also be less likely to believe that other equally good answers were possible. As a participant you are not limited to offering answers; you may ask questions, too. ∎

By and About Sigmund Freud

(1856–1939)

W. H. Auden said of Freud:

> to us he is no more a person
> now but a whole climate of opinion.

Sigmund Freud explored the effects of unconscious mental forces on conscious life. He wrote:

> The unconscious must be accepted as the general basis of the psychic life. The unconscious is the larger circle which includes the smaller circle of the conscious; everything conscious has a preliminary unconscious stage. . . . The unconscious is the true psychic reality; *in its inner nature it is just as much unknown to us as the reality of the external world, and it is just as imperfectly communicated to us by the data of consciousness as is the external world by the reports of our sense organs.*

Freud developed his psychoanalytic technique from self-analysis and his treatment of hysterical patients in Vienna at the turn of the century. A student of literature as well as a scientist, he was sensitive to the power of language.

> Words and magic were in the beginning one and the same thing, and even today words retain much of their magical power. By words one of us can give to another the greatest happiness or bring about utter despair; by words the teacher imparts his knowledge to the student; by words the orator sweeps his audience with him and determines its judgments and decisions. Words call forth emotions and are universally the means by which we influence our fellow-creatures. Therefore let us not despise the use of words in psychotherapy.

Freud held that a strong desire for aggression is part of our instinctual endowment:

> Men are not gentle, friendly creatures wishing for love, who simply defend themselves if they are attacked. . . . Their neighbor is to them not only a possible helper or sexual object, but also a

temptation to them to gratify their aggressiveness on him, to exploit his capacity for work without recompense, to use him sexually without his consent, to seize his possessions, to humiliate him, to cause him pain, to torture and kill him. *Homo homini lupus* [man is a wolf to man]; who has the courage to dispute it in the face of all the evidence in his own life and in history?

Yet he insisted:

It is no part of our intention to deny the nobility in human nature, nor have we ever done anything to disparage its value. On the contrary, I show you not only the evil wishes which are censored but also the censorship which suppresses them and makes them unrecognizable. We dwell upon the evil in human beings with the greater emphasis only because others deny it, thereby making the mental life of mankind not indeed better, but incomprehensible. If we give up the one-sided ethical valuation then, we are sure to find the truer formula for the relation of evil to good in human nature.

In 1932, the League of Nations asked Albert Einstein to choose a problem of interest to him and to exchange views with someone about it. Einstein chose "Is there any way of delivering mankind from the menace of war?" as his problem and Sigmund Freud as his correspondent. In his letter to Freud, Einstein said that one way of eliminating war was to establish a supranational organization with the authority to settle disputes between nations and the power to enforce its decisions. But Einstein acknowledged that this solution dealt only with the administrative aspect of the problem, and that international security could never be achieved until more was known about human psychology. Must right always be supported by might? Why were men eager to go to war and sacrifice their lives? Was everyone susceptible to feelings of hate and destructiveness? It was to these questions Freud addressed himself in his reply.

Why War?

Sigmund Freud

Vienna, September, 1932.

Dear Professor Einstein,

When I heard that you intended to invite me to an exchange of views on some subject that interested you and that seemed to deserve the interest of others besides yourself, I readily agreed. I expected you to choose a problem on the frontiers of what is knowable today, a problem to which each of us, a physicist and a psychologist, might have our own particular angle of approach and where we might come together from different directions upon the same ground. You have taken me by surprise, however, by posing the question of what can be done to protect mankind from the curse of war. I was scared at first by the thought of my—I had almost written "our"—incapacity for dealing with what seemed to be a practical problem, a concern for statesmen. But I then realized that you had raised the question not as a natural scientist and physicist but as a philanthropist: you were following the promptings of the

League of Nations just as Fridtjof Nansen, the polar explorer, took on the work of bringing help to the starving and homeless victims of the World War. I reflected, moreover, that I was not being asked to make practical proposals but only to set out the problem of avoiding war as it appears to a psychological observer. Here again you yourself have said almost all there is to say on the subject. But though you have taken the wind out of my sails I shall be glad to follow in your wake and content myself with confirming all you have said by amplifying it to the best of my knowledge—or conjecture.

You begin with the relation between Right and Might. There can be no doubt that that is the correct starting-point for our investigation. But may I replace the word "might" by the balder and harsher word "violence"? Today right and violence appear to us as antitheses. It can easily be shown, however, that the one has developed out of the other; and, if we go back to the earliest beginnings and see how that first came about, the problem is easily solved. You must forgive me if in what follows I go over familiar and commonly accepted ground as though it were new, but the thread of my argument requires it.

It is a general principle, then, that conflicts of interest between men are settled by the use of violence. This is true of the whole animal kingdom, from which men have no business to exclude themselves. In the case of men, no doubt, conflicts of *opinion* occur as well which may reach the highest pitch of abstraction and which seem to demand some other technique for their settlement. That, however, is a later complication. To begin with, in a small human horde,* it was superior muscular strength which decided who owned things or whose will should

---

* *horde.* A primitive social unit made up of a number of families.

prevail. Muscular strength was soon supplemented and replaced by the use of tools: the winner was the one who had the better weapons or who used them the more skillfully. From the moment at which weapons were introduced, intellectual superiority already began to replace brute muscular strength; but the final purpose of the fight remained the same—one side or the other was to be compelled to abandon his claim or his objection by the damage inflicted on him and by the crippling of his strength. That purpose was most completely achieved if the victor's violence eliminated his opponent permanently—that is to say, killed him. This had two advantages: he could not renew his opposition and his fate deterred others from following his example. In addition to this, killing an enemy satisfied an instinctual inclination which I shall have to mention later. The intention to kill might be countered by a reflection that the enemy could be employed in performing useful services if he were left alive in an intimidated condition. In that case the victor's violence was content with subjugating him instead of killing him. This was a first beginning of the idea of sparing an enemy's life, but thereafter the victor had to reckon with his defeated opponent's lurking thirst for revenge and sacrificed some of his own security.

Such, then, was the original state of things: domination by whoever had the greater might—domination by brute violence or by violence supported by intellect. As we know, this régime was altered in the course of evolution. There was a path that led from violence to right or law. What was that path? It is my belief that there was only one: the path which led by way of the fact that the superior strength of a single individual could be rivaled by the union of several weak ones. *"L'union fait la force."** Violence could be broken by union, and the

---

* *L'union fait la force.* In union there is strength.

power of those who were united now represented law in contrast to the violence of the single individual. Thus we see that
right is the might of a community. It is still violence, ready to
be directed against any individual who resists it; it works by the
same methods and follows the same purposes. The only real
difference lies in the fact that what prevails is no longer the
violence of an individual but that of a community. But in order
that the transition from violence to this new right or justice
may be effected, one psychological condition must be fulfilled.
The union of the majority must be a stable and lasting one. If
it were only brought about for the purpose of combating a
single dominant individual and were dissolved after his defeat,
nothing would have been accomplished. The next person who
thought himself superior in strength would once more seek to
set up a dominion by violence and the game would be repeated
ad infinitum. The community must be maintained permanently, must be organized, must draw up regulations to anticipate
the risk of rebellion and must institute authorities to see that
those regulations—the laws—are respected and to superintend
the execution of legal acts of violence. The recognition of a
community of interests such as these leads to the growth of
emotional ties between the members of a united group of
people—communal feelings which are the true source of its
strength.

Here, I believe, we already have all the essentials: violence
overcome by the transference of power to a larger unity, which
is held together by emotional ties between its members. What
remains to be said is no more than an expansion and a repetition of this.

The situation is simple so long as the community consists
only of a number of equally strong individuals. The laws of
such an association will determine the extent to which, if the

security of communal life is to be guaranteed, each individual must surrender his personal liberty to turn his strength to violent uses. But a state of rest of that kind is only theoretically conceivable. In actuality the position is complicated by the fact that from its very beginning the community comprises elements of unequal strength—men and women, parents and children—and soon, as a result of war and conquest, it also comes to include victors and vanquished, who turn into masters and slaves. The justice of the community then becomes an expression of the unequal degrees of power obtaining within it; the laws are made by and for the ruling members and find little room for the rights of those in subjection. From that time forward there are two factors at work in the community which are sources of unrest over matters of law but tend at the same time to a further growth of law. First, attempts are made by certain of the rulers to set themselves above the prohibitions which apply to everyone—they seek, that is, to go back from a dominion of law to a dominion of violence. Secondly, the oppressed members of the group make constant efforts to obtain more power and to have any changes that are brought about in that direction recognized in the laws—they press forward, that is, from unequal justice to equal justice for all. This second tendency becomes especially important if a real shift of power occurs within a community, as may happen as a result of a number of historical factors. In that case right may gradually adapt itself to the new distribution of power; or, as is more frequent, the ruling class is unwilling to recognize the change, and rebellion and civil war follow, with a temporary suspension of law and new attempts at a solution by violence, ending in the establishment of a fresh rule of law. There is yet another source from which modifications of law may arise, and one of which the expression is invariably peaceful: it lies in the cultural transformation of the members of the community. . . .

I can now proceed to add a gloss to another of your remarks. You express astonishment at the fact that it is so easy to make men enthusiastic about a war and add your suspicions that there is something at work in them—an instinct for hatred and destruction—which goes halfway to meet the efforts of the warmongers. Once again, I can only express my entire agreement. We believe in the existence of an instinct of that kind and have in fact been occupied during the last few years in studying its manifestations. Will you allow me to take this opportunity of putting before you a portion of the theory of the instincts which, after much tentative groping and many fluctuations of opinion, has been reached by workers in the field of psychoanalysis?

According to our hypothesis human instincts are of only two kinds: those which seek to preserve and unite—which we call "erotic," exactly in the sense in which Plato uses the word "Eros" in his *Symposium,* or "sexual," with a deliberate extension of the popular conception of "sexuality"—and those which seek to destroy and kill and which we group together as the aggressive or destructive instinct. As you see, this is in fact no more than a theoretical clarification of the universally familiar opposition between Love and Hate which may perhaps have some fundamental relation to the polarity of attraction and repulsion that plays a part in your own field of knowledge. But we must not be too hasty in introducing ethical judgments of good and evil. Neither of these instincts is any less essential than the other; the phenomena of life arise from the concurrent or mutually opposing action of both. Now it seems as though an instinct of the one sort can scarcely ever operate in isolation; it is always accompanied—or, as we say, alloyed—with a certain quota from the other side, which modifies its aim or is, in some cases, what enables it to achieve that aim. Thus, for instance, the instinct of self-preservation is certainly of an erotic kind, but it must nevertheless have aggressiveness at its disposal if it is to fulfill its purpose. So, too, the instinct of love, when it is directed towards an object, stands in need of some contribution from the instinct for mastery if it is in any way to obtain possession of that object. The difficulty of isolating the two classes of instinct in their actual manifestations is indeed what has so long prevented us from recognizing them.

If you will follow me a little further, you will see that human actions are subject to another complication of a different kind. It is very rarely that an action is the work of a *single* instinctual impulse (which must in itself be compounded of Eros and destructiveness). In order to make an action possible there must be as a rule a combination of such compounded motives. This was perceived long ago by a specialist in your own subject, a Professor G. C. Lichtenberg who taught physics at Göttingen during our classical age—though perhaps he was even more remarkable as a psychologist than as a physicist. He invented a Compass of Motives, for he wrote: "The motives that lead us to do anything might be arranged like the thirty-two winds and might be given names in a similar way: for instance, 'bread-bread-fame' or 'fame-fame-bread'." So that when human beings are incited to war they may have a whole number of motives for assenting—some noble and some base, some which are openly declared and others which are never mentioned. There is no need to enumerate them all. A lust for aggression and destruction is certainly among them: the countless cruelties in history and in our everyday lives vouch for its existence and its strength. The satisfaction of these destructive impulses is of course facilitated by their admixture with others of an erotic and idealistic kind. When we read of the atrocities of the past, it sometimes seems as though the idealistic motives served only as an excuse for the destructive appetites; and sometimes—in the case, for instance, of the cruelties of the

Inquisition—it seems as though the idealistic motives had pushed themselves forward in consciousness, while the destructive ones lent them an unconscious reinforcement. Both may be true.

I fear I may be abusing your interest, which is after all concerned with the prevention of war and not with our theories. Nevertheless I should like to linger for a moment over our destructive instinct, whose popularity is by no means equal to its importance. As a result of a little speculation, we have come to suppose that this instinct is at work in every living creature and is striving to bring it to ruin and to reduce life to its original condition of inanimate matter. Thus it quite seriously deserves to be called a death instinct, while the erotic instincts represent the effort to live. The death instinct turns into the destructive instinct when, with the help of special organs, it is directed outwards, on to objects. The organism preserves its own life, so to say, by destroying an extraneous one. Some portion of the death instinct, however, remains operative *within* the organism, and we have sought to trace quite a number of normal and pathological phenomena to this internalization of the destructive instinct. We have even been guilty of the heresy of attributing the origin of conscience to this diversion inwards of aggressiveness. You will notice that it is by no means a trivial matter if this process is carried too far: it is positively unhealthy. On the other hand if these forces are turned to destruction in the external world, the organism will be relieved and the effect must be beneficial. This would serve as a biological justification for all the ugly and dangerous impulses against which we are struggling. It must be admitted that they stand nearer to Nature than does our resistance to them for which an explanation also needs to be found. It may perhaps seem to you as though our theories are a kind of mythology and, in the present case, not even an agreeable one. But does not every science come in the end to a kind of mythology like this? Cannot the same be said today of your own Physics?

For our immediate purpose then, this much follows from what has been said: there is no use in trying to get rid of men's aggressive inclinations. We are told that in certain happy regions of the earth, where nature provides in abundance everything that man requires, there are races whose life is passed in tranquillity and who know neither coercion nor aggression. I can scarcely believe it and I should be glad to hear more of these fortunate beings. The Russian Communists, too, hope to be able to cause human aggressiveness to disappear by guaranteeing the satisfaction of all material needs and by establishing equality in other respects among all the members of the community. That, in my opinion, is an illusion. They themselves are armed today with the most scrupulous care and not the least important of the methods by which they keep their supporters together is hatred of everyone beyond their frontiers. In any case, as you yourself have remarked, there is no question of getting rid entirely of human aggressive impulses; it is enough to try to divert them to such an extent that they need not find expression in war.

Our mythological theory of instincts makes it easy for us to find a formula for *indirect* methods of combating war. If willingness to engage in war is an effect of the destructive instinct, the most obvious plan will be to bring Eros, its antagonist, into play against it. Anything that encourages the growth of emotional ties between men must operate against war. These ties may be of two kinds. In the first place they may be relations resembling those towards a loved object, though without having a sexual aim. There is no need for psychoanalysis to be ashamed to speak of love in this connection, for religion itself uses the same words: "Thou shalt love thy neighbor as thyself."

This, however, is more easily said than done. The second kind of emotional tie is by means of identification. Whatever leads men to share important interests produces this community of feeling, these identifications. And the structure of human society is to a large extent based on them. . . .

The result, as you see, is not very fruitful when an unworldly theoretician is called in to advise on an urgent practical problem. It is a better plan to devote oneself in every particular case to meeting the danger with whatever means lie to hand. I should like, however, to discuss one more question, which you do not mention in your letter but which specially interests me. Why do you and I and so many other people rebel so violently against war? Why do we not accept it as another of the many painful calamities of life? After all, it seems to be quite a natural thing, to have a good biological basis and in practice to be scarcely avoidable. There is no need to be shocked at my raising this question. For the purpose of an investigation such as this, one may perhaps be allowed to wear a mask of assumed detachment. The answer to my question will be that we react to war in this way because everyone has a right to his own life, because war puts an end to human lives that are full of hope, because it brings individual men into humiliating situations, because it compels them against their will to murder other men, and because it destroys precious material objects which have been produced by the labors of humanity. Other reasons besides might be given, such as that in its present-day form war is no longer an opportunity for achieving the old ideals of heroism and that owing to the perfection of instruments of destruction a future war might involve the extermination of one or perhaps both of the antagonists. All this is true, and so incontestably true that one can only feel astonished that the waging of war has not yet been unanimously repudiated. No doubt debate is possible upon one or two of these points. It may be questioned whether a community ought not to have a right to dispose of individual lives; every war is not open to condemnation to an equal degree; so long as there exist countries and nations that are prepared for the ruthless destruction of others, those others must be armed for war. But I will not linger over any of these issues; they are not what you want to discuss with me, and I have something different in mind. It is my opinion that the main reason why we rebel against war is that we cannot help doing so. We are pacifists because we are obliged to be for organic reasons. And we then find no difficulty in producing arguments to justify our attitude. . . .

I trust you will forgive me if what I have said has disappointed you, and I remain, with kindest regards,

Sincerely yours,
SIGM. FREUD

Interpretive Questions

1. Is it possible, according to Freud, for people to make changes in their society without recourse to violence?

2. What happens to the aggressive instinct when people unite to form a lawful society?

3. How does the violence of the community differ from the violence of the individual?

4. Is one of the two basic instincts stronger than the other? Better than the other? More natural than the other?

5. Is Freud hopeful that war can be avoided?

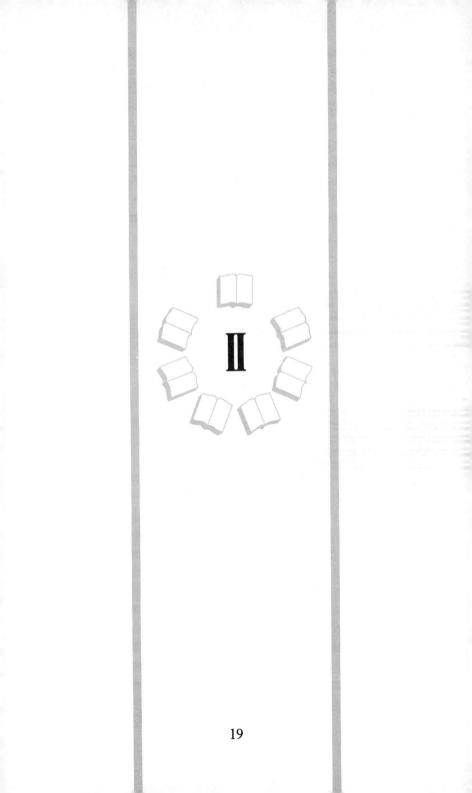

II

Great Writers

Reading what Thucydides has to say about the
relationship between great powers and their
satellites, or what Thomas Hobbes has to say
about human nature and government, or what
John Dewey has to say about the formation of
habits can change the way we look at things. We
may not agree with these writers, but as we come
to understand what they say, it is unlikely that we
will ever again think about foreign policy or
government or habit in quite the same way.

This kind of writing is rare. The depth of thought it conveys often makes it difficult to understand. We need to work hard to make a great writer's ideas our own. For making an idea our own is not a simple matter of agreement or memorization. It means becoming so familiar with someone else's thought that we can turn it around, consider it from different angles, and then decide how it fits with our own ideas.

Great writers give us the opportunity to form our own opinions on the basis of the most profound thinking that has ever been expressed. They require us to think about what it means to live in the world and about what we are and what we hope to become. As we make an effort to understand great writers, we find ourselves seeing further, as Isaac Newton put it, "by standing upon the shoulders of giants." ∎

By and About Thucydides

(471–400? B.C.)

Thomas Babington Macaulay, the nineteenth-century English historian, wrote in his diary: "This day I finished Thucydides, after reading him with inexpressible interest and admiration. He is the greatest historian who ever lived."

Thucydides, an exiled Athenian general, based his *History of the Peloponnesian War* on personal observation and the eyewitness accounts of Athenians and Spartans alike. He says that he wrote his history

> in the belief that it was going to be a great war and more worth writing about than any of those which had taken place in the past. My belief was based on the fact that the two sides were at the very height of their power and preparedness, and I saw, too, that the rest of the Hellenic world was committed to one side or the other; even those who were not immediately engaged were deliberating on the courses which they were to take later. This was the greatest disturbance in the history of the Hellenes, affecting also a large part of the non-Hellenic world, and indeed, I might also say, the whole of mankind.

He speaks of his method of writing history:

> In this history I have made use of set speeches, some of which were delivered just before, and others during, the war. I have found it difficult to remember the precise words used in the speeches which I listened to myself, and my various informants have experienced the same difficulty; so my method has been, while keeping as closely as possible to the general sense of the words that were actually used, to make the speakers say what, in my opinion, was called for by each situation.
>
> With regard to my factual reporting of the events of the war, I have made it a principle not to write down the first story that came my way and not even to be guided by my own general impressions; either I was present myself at the events which I have described or else I heard of them from eyewitnesses whose reports I have checked with as much thoroughness as possible. Not that

even so the truth was easy to discover: different eyewitnesses give different accounts of the same events, speaking out of partiality for one side or the other or else from imperfect memories.

Thucydides notes what happens to words in wartime:

To fit in with the change of events, words, too, had to change their usual meanings. What used to be described as a thoughtless act of aggression was now regarded as the courage one would expect to find in a party member; to think of the future and wait was merely another way of saying one was a coward; any idea of moderation was just an attempt to disguise one's unmanly character; ability to understand a question from all sides meant that one was totally unfitted for action. Fanatical enthusiasm was the mark of a real man, and to plot against an enemy behind his back was perfectly legitimate self-defense.

He extols patriotism:

Your country has a right to your services in sustaining the glories of her position. These are a common source of pride to you all, and you cannot decline the burdens of empire and still expect to share its honors.

He professes his faith in the democracy of his time:

It will be said, perhaps, that democracy is neither wise nor equitable, but that the holders of property are also the best fitted to rule. I say, on the contrary, first, that the word *demos,* or people, includes the whole state, oligarchy only a part; next, that if the best guardians of property are the rich, and the best counsellors the wise, none can hear and decide so well as the many; and that all these talents, severally and collectively, have their just place in a democracy.

Thucydides' History of the Peloponnesian War *describes the conflict between Athens and Sparta that took place between 431 and 404 B.C. and involved most of the Greek city-states on one side or the other. Melos, a small island off the southeastern coast of Greece, tried to remain independent and neutral, resisting an Athenian attempt to make it a tributary. Athens then sent a second expedition to subjugate the island, or at least to force it into an alliance. Before giving the order to attack, the Athenian generals sent representatives to negotiate with the Melians. The meeting dealt with the issue of whether a great power should be swayed by anything except self-interest in dealing with a smaller power.*

The Melian Dialogue

Thucydides

The next summer the Athenians made an expedition against the isle of Melos. The Melians are a colony of Lacedaemon that would not submit to the Athenians like the other islanders and at first remained neutral and took no part in the struggle, but afterwards, upon the Athenians using violence and plundering their territory, assumed an attitude of open hostility. The Athenian generals encamped in their territory with their army, and before doing any harm to their land sent envoys to negotiate. These the Melians did not bring before the people, but told them to state the object of their mission to the magistrates and the council. The Athenian envoys then said:

ATHENIANS: As we are not to speak to the people, for fear that if we made a single speech without interruption we might deceive them with attractive arguments to which there was no chance of replying—we realize that this is the meaning of our being brought before your ruling body—we suggest that you

---

*A selection from *The History of the Peloponnesian War*.

who sit here should make security doubly sure. Let us have no long speeches from you either, but deal separately with each point, and take up at once any statement of which you disapprove, and criticize it.

MELIANS: We have no objection to your reasonable suggestion that we should put our respective points of view quietly to each other, but the military preparations which you have already made seem inconsistent with it. We see that you have come to be yourselves the judges of the debate, and that its natural conclusion for us will be slavery if you convince us, and war if we get the better of the argument and therefore refuse to submit.

ATHENIANS: If you have met us in order to make surmises about the future, or for any other purpose than to look existing facts in the face and to discuss the safety of your city on this basis, we will break off the conversations; otherwise, we are ready to speak.

MELIANS: In our position it is natural and excusable to explore many ideas and arguments. But the problem that has brought us here is our security, so, if you think fit, let the discussion follow the line you propose.

ATHENIANS: Then we will not make a long and unconvincing speech, full of fine phrases, to prove that our victory over Persia justifies our empire, or that we are now attacking you because you have wronged us, and we ask you not to expect to convince us by saying that you have not injured us, or that, though a colony of Lacedaemon, you did not join her. Let each of us say what we really think and reach a practical agreement. You know and we know, as practical men, that the question of justice arises only between parties equal in strength, and that the strong do what they can, and the weak submit.

MELIANS: As you ignore justice and have made self-interest the basis of discussion, we must take the same ground, and we say that in our opinion it is in your interest to maintain a principle which is for the good of all—that anyone in danger should have just and equitable treatment and any advantage, even if not strictly his due, which he can secure by persuasion. This is your interest as much as ours, for your fall would involve you in a crushing punishment that would be a lesson to the world.

ATHENIANS: We have no apprehensions about the fate of our empire, if it did fall; those who rule other peoples, like the Lacedaemonians, are not formidable to a defeated enemy. Nor is it the Lacedaemonians with whom we are now contending: the danger is from subjects who of themselves may attack and conquer their rulers. But leave that danger to us to face. At the moment we shall prove that we have come in the interest of our empire and that in what we shall say we are seeking the safety of your state; for we wish you to become our subjects with least trouble to ourselves, and we would like you to survive in our interests as well as your own.

MELIANS: It may be your interest to be our masters; how can it be ours to be your slaves?

ATHENIANS: By submitting you would avoid a terrible fate, and we should gain by not destroying you.

MELIANS: Would you not agree to an arrangement under which we should keep out of the war, and be your friends instead of your enemies, but neutral?

ATHENIANS: No; your hostility injures us less than your friendship. That, to our subjects, is an illustration of our weakness, while your hatred exhibits our power.

MELIANS: Is this the construction which your subjects put on it? Do they not distinguish between states in which you have no concern, and peoples who are most of them your colonies, and some conquered rebels?

ATHENIANS: They think that one nation has as good rights

as another, but that some survive because they are strong and we are afraid to attack them. So, apart from the addition to our empire, your subjection would give us security: the fact that you are islanders (and weaker than others) makes it the more important that you should not get the better of the mistress of the sea.

MELIANS: But do you see no safety in our neutrality? You debar us from the plea of justice and press us to submit to your interests, so we must expound our own, and try to convince you, if the two happen to coincide. Will you not make enemies of all neutral Powers when they see your conduct and reflect that some day you will attack them? Will not your action strengthen your existing opponents, and induce those who would otherwise never be your enemies to become so against their will?

ATHENIANS: No. The mainland states, secure in their freedom, will be slow to take defensive measures against us, and we do not consider them so formidable as independent island powers like yourselves, or subjects already smarting under our yoke. These are most likely to take a thoughtless step and bring themselves and us into obvious danger.

MELIANS: Surely then, if you are ready to risk so much to maintain your empire, and the enslaved peoples so much to escape from it, it would be criminal cowardice in us, who are still free, not to take any and every measure before submitting to slavery?

ATHENIANS: No, if you reflect calmly: for this is not a competition in heroism between equals, where your honor is at stake, but a question of self-preservation, to save you from a struggle with a far stronger Power.

MELIANS: Still, we know that in war fortune is more impartial than the disproportion in numbers might lead one to expect. If we submit at once, our position is desperate; if we fight, there is still a hope that we shall stand secure.

ATHENIANS: Hope encourages men to take risks; men in a strong position may follow her without ruin, if not without loss. But when they stake all that they have to the last coin (for she is a spendthrift), she reveals her real self in the hour of failure, and when her nature is known she leaves them without means of self-protection. You are weak, your future hangs on a turn of the scales; avoid the mistake most men make, who might save themselves by human means, and then, when visible hopes desert them, in their extremity turn to the invisible—prophecies and oracles and all those things which delude men with hopes, to their destruction.

MELIANS: We too, you can be sure, realize the difficulty of struggling against your power and against Fortune if she is not impartial. Still we trust that Heaven will not allow us to be worsted by Fortune, for in this quarrel we are right and you are wrong. Besides, we expect the support of Lacedaemon to supply the deficiencies in our strength, for she is bound to help us as her kinsmen, if for no other reason, and from a sense of honor. So our confidence is not entirely unreasonable.

ATHENIANS: As for divine favor, we think that we can count on it as much as you, for neither our claims nor our actions are inconsistent with what men believe about Heaven or desire for themselves. We believe that Heaven, and we know that men, by a natural law, always rule where they are stronger. We did not make that law nor were we the first to act on it; we found it existing, and it will exist forever, after we are gone; and we know that you and anyone else as strong as we are would do as we do. As to your expectations from Lacedaemon and your belief that she will help you from a sense of honor, we congratulate you on your innocence but we do not admire your folly. So far as they themselves and their national traditions are concerned, the Lacedaemonians are a highly virtuous people; as for their behavior to others, much might be said, but we can put it shortly by saying that, most obviously of all people we know, they identify their interests with justice and the pleasantest course with honor. Such principles do not favor your present irrational hopes of deliverance.

MELIANS: That is the chief reason why we have confidence in them now; in their own interest they will not wish to betray their own colonists and so help their enemies and destroy the confidence that their friends in Greece feel in them.

ATHENIANS: Apparently you do not realize that safety and self-interest go together, while the path of justice and honor is dangerous; and danger is a risk which the Lacedaemonians are little inclined to run.

MELIANS: Our view is that they would be more likely to run a risk in our case, and would regard it as less hazardous, because our nearness to Peloponnese makes it easier for them to act and our kinship gives them more confidence in us than in others.

ATHENIANS: Yes, but an intending ally looks not to the goodwill of those who invoke his aid but to marked superiority of real power, and of none is this truer than of the Lacedaemonians. They mistrust their own resources and attack their neighbors only when they have numerous allies, so it is not likely that, while we are masters of the sea, they would cross it to an island.

MELIANS: They might send others. The sea of Crete is large, and this will make it more difficult for its masters to capture hostile ships than for these to elude them safely. If they failed by sea, they would attack your country and those of your allies whom Brasidas* did not reach; and then you will

---

* *Brasidas.* A courageous and aggressive Spartan general who won many victories against the Athenians and their allies before he was killed in the tenth year of the war.

have to fight not against a country in which you have no concern, but for your own country and your allies' lands.

ATHENIANS: Here experience may teach you like others, and you will learn that Athens has never abandoned a siege from fear of another foe. You said that you proposed to discuss the safety of your city, but we observe that in all your speeches you have never said a word on which any reasonable expectation of it could be founded. Your strength lies in deferred hopes; in comparison with the forces now arrayed against you, your resources are too small for any hope of success. You will show a great want of judgment if you do not come to a more reasonable decision after we have withdrawn. Surely you will not fall back on the idea of honor, which has been the ruin of so many when danger and disgrace were staring them in the face. How often, when men have seen the fate to which they were tending, have they been enslaved by a phrase and drawn by the power of this seductive word to fall of their own free will into irreparable disaster, bringing on themselves by their folly a greater dishonor than fortune could inflict! If you are wise, you will avoid that fate. The greatest of cities makes you a fair offer, to keep your own land and become her tributary ally: there is no dishonor in that. The choice between war and safety is given you; do not obstinately take the worse alternative. The most successful people are those who stand up to their equals, behave properly to their superiors, and treat their inferiors fairly. Think it over when we withdraw, and reflect once and again that you have only one country, and that its prosperity or ruin depends on one decision.

The Athenians now withdrew from the conference; and the Melians, left to themselves, came to a decision corresponding with what they had maintained in the discussion, and answered, "Our resolution, Athenians, is unaltered. We will not in a moment deprive of freedom a city that has existed for seven hundred years; we put our trust in the fortune by which the gods have preserved it until now, and in the help of men, that is, of the Lacedaemonians; and so we will try and save ourselves. Meanwhile we invite you to allow us to be friends to you and foes to neither party, and to retire from our country after making such a treaty as shall seem fit to us both."

Such was the answer of the Melians. The Athenians broke up the conference saying, "To judge from your decision, you are unique in regarding the future as more certain than the present and in allowing your wishes to convert the unseen into reality; and as you have staked most on, and trusted most in, the Lacedaemonians, your fortune, and your hopes, so will you be most completely deceived."

The Athenian envoys now returned to the army; and as the Melians showed no signs of yielding, the generals at once began hostilities, and drew a line of circumvallation round the Melians, dividing the work among the different states. Subsequently the Athenians returned with most of their army, leaving behind them a certain number of their own citizens and of the allies to keep guard by land and sea. The force thus left stayed on and besieged the place.

Meanwhile the Athenians at Pylos took so much plunder from the Lacedaemonians that the latter, although they still refrained from breaking off the treaty and going to war with Athens, proclaimed that any of their people that chose might plunder the Athenians. The Corinthians also commenced hostilities with the Athenians for private quarrels of their own; but the rest of the Peloponnesians stayed quiet. Meanwhile the Melians in a night attack took the part of the Athenian lines opposite the market, killed some of its garrison, and brought in corn and as many useful stores as they could. Then, retiring, they remained inactive, while the Athenians took measures to keep better guard in future.

Summer was now over. The next winter the Lacedaemonians intended to invade the Argive territory, but on arriving at the frontier found the sacrifices for crossing unfavorable, and went back again. This intention of theirs made the Argives suspicious of certain of their fellow citizens, some of whom they arrested; others, however, escaped them. About the same time the Melians again took another part of the Athenian lines which were but feebly garrisoned. In consequence reinforcements were sent from Athens, and the siege was now pressed vigorously; there was some treachery in the town, and the Melians surrendered at discretion to the Athenians, who put to death all the grown men whom they took, and sold the women and children for slaves; subsequently they sent out five hundred settlers and colonized the island.

Interpretive Questions

1. Does Thucydides think the Melians should have accepted the Athenians' offer?

2. Does Thucydides believe that justice has no place in dealings between nations that are unequal in power?

3. Why do the Athenians want to restrict their discussion with the Melians to matters of mutual self-interest and omit all arguments based on gratitude, honor, or justice?

4. Do the Melians have a keener sense of honor than the Athenians do, or are they merely using honor as a ploy for getting out of a tight spot?

5. If the Melians believe the debate can only result in either war or slavery, why do they agree to debate?

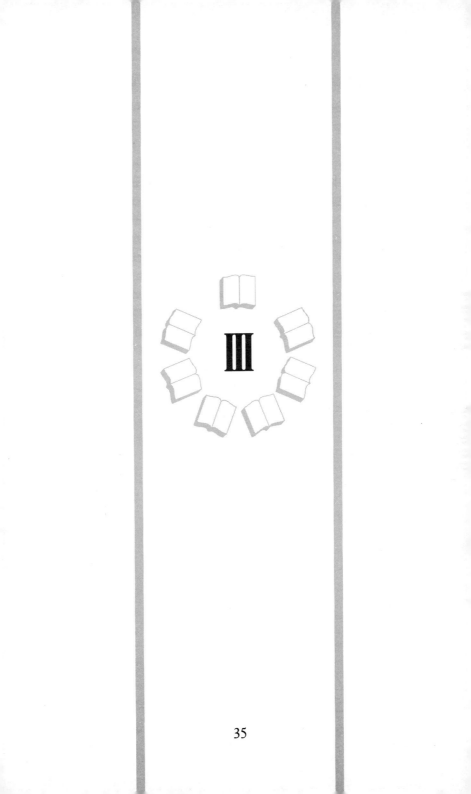

III

By and About William James

(1842–1910)

William James, the distinguished American psychologist and philosopher, was the elder brother of novelist Henry James.

On the need to risk ourselves:

> So far as man stands for anything, and is productive or originative at all, his entire vital function may be said to have to deal with maybes. Not a victory is gained, not a deed of faithfulness or courage is done, except upon a maybe; not a service, not a sally of generosity, not a scientific exploration or experiment or text-book that may not be a mistake. It is only by risking our persons from one hour to another that we live at all. And often enough our faith beforehand in an uncertified result *is the only thing that makes the result come true.*

On point of view:

> We can act *as if* there were a God; feel *as if* we were free; consider Nature *as if* she were full of special designs; lay plans *as if* we were to be immortal; and we find then that these words do make a genuine difference in our moral life.

On conviction:

> I cannot understand the willingness to act, no matter how we feel, without the belief that acts are really good and bad. I cannot understand the belief that an act is bad, without regret at its happening. I cannot understand regret without the admission of real, genuine possibilities in the world. Only *then* is it other than a mockery to feel, after we have failed to do our best, that an irreparable opportunity is gone from the universe, the loss of which it must forever after mourn.

William James says, "In its widest possible sense . . . a man's Me is the sum total of all he CAN *call his, not only his body and his psychic powers, but his clothes and his house, his wife and children, his ancestors and friends, his reputation and works, his lands and horses, and yacht and bank account. All these things give him the same emotions. If they wax and prosper, he feels triumphant; if they dwindle and die away, he feels cast down—not necessarily in the same degree for each thing, but in much the same way for all." To understand the Me in this widest sense, James has us examine the material me, the social me, and the spiritual me.*

The material me consists of body and clothing, and widens out to include family, home, and property. "We all have a blind impulse," James says, "to watch over our body, to deck it with clothing of an ornamental sort, to cherish parents, wife, and babes, and to find ourselves a house of our own which we may live in and 'improve.' "

By the spiritual me, James says, "I mean . . . the entire collection of my states of consciousness, my psychic faculties and dispositions taken concretely. This collection can at any moment become an object to my thought at that moment and awaken emotions like those awakened by any of the other portions of the Me. When we think *of ourselves as thinkers, all the other ingredients of our Me seem relatively external possessions."*

In our selection, James discusses the third me, the social me.

The Social Me

William James

A man's social me is the recognition which he gets from his mates. We are not only gregarious animals, liking to be in sight of our fellows, but we have an innate propensity to get ourselves noticed, and noticed favorably, by our kind. No more fiendish punishment could be devised, were such a thing physically possible, than that one should be turned loose in society and remain absolutely unnoticed by all the members thereof. If no one turned round when we entered, answered when we spoke, or minded what we did, but if every person we met "cut us dead," and acted as if we were nonexisting things, a kind of rage and impotent despair would ere long well up in us, from which the cruellest bodily tortures would be a relief; for these would make us feel that, however bad might be our plight, we had not sunk to such a depth as to be unworthy of attention at all.

Properly speaking, *a man has as many social selves as there are individuals who recognize him* and carry an image of him

---

*A selection from *Psychology: Briefer Course.*

in their mind. To wound any one of these his images is to wound him. But as the individuals who carry the images fall naturally into two classes, we may practically say that he has as many different social selves as there are distinct *groups* of persons about whose opinion he cares. He generally shows a different side of himself to each of these different groups. Many a youth who is demure enough before his parents and teachers, swears and swaggers like a pirate among his "tough" young friends. We do not show ourselves to our children as to our club companions, to our customers as to the laborers we employ, to our own masters and employers as to our intimate friends. From this there results what practically is a division of the man into several selves; and this may be a discordant splitting, as where one is afraid to let one set of his acquaintances know him as he is elsewhere; or it may be a perfectly harmonious division of labor, as where one tender to his children is stern to the soldiers or prisoners under his command.

The most peculiar social self which one is apt to have is in the mind of the person one is in love with. The good or bad fortunes of this self cause the most intense elation and dejection—unreasonable enough as measured by every other standard than that of the organic feeling of the individual. To his own consciousness he *is* not, so long as this particular social self fails to get recognition, and when it is recognized his contentment passes all bounds.

A man's *fame,* good or bad, and his *honor* or dishonor are names for one of his social selves. The particular social self of a man called his honor is usually the result of one of those splittings of which we have spoken. It is his image in the eyes of his own "set," which exalts or condemns him as he conforms or not to certain requirements that may not be made of one in another walk of life. Thus a layman may abandon a city infected with cholera, but a priest or a doctor would think such an act incompatible with his honor. A soldier's honor requires him to fight or to die under circumstances where another man can apologize or run away with no stain upon his social self. A judge, a statesman, are in like manner debarred by the honor of their cloth from entering into pecuniary relations perfectly honorable to persons in private life. Nothing is commoner than to hear people discriminate between their different selves of this sort: "As a man I pity you, but as an official I must show you no mercy"; "As a politician I regard him as an ally, but as a moralist I loathe him"; etc., etc. What may be called "club-opinion" is one of the very strongest forces in life. The thief must not steal from other thieves; the gambler must pay his gambling debts, though he pay no other debts in the world. The code of honor of fashionable society has throughout history been full of permissions as well as of vetoes, the only reason for following either of which is that so we best serve one of our social selves. You must not lie in general, but you may lie as much as you please if asked about your relations with a lady; you must accept a challenge from an equal, but if challenged by an inferior you may laugh him to scorn: these are examples of what is meant.

📖

Interpretive Questions

1. Can someone have a personal code of honor, according to James?

2. Is "recognition" the same as acceptance by some group?

3. Who is more important in forming the social me: oneself or others?

4. Is there a "real me" apart from my social selves?

5. Does a hermit have a social self?

contentmen[...]
A man's [...]
names for [...]
a man call[...]
splittings o[...]
of his own[...]
forms or n[...]
one in and[...]
infected w[...]
an act inc[...]
him to fig[...]
can apol[...]
A judge, [...]
of their [...]
honorab[...]
than to l[...]
of this s[...]
you no[...]
as a m[...]
"club-c[...]

*Does James [...]
standard of [...]*

*Is good and [...]
attempt to [...]
group or a[...]*

*Why do our [...]
different stan[...]*

*Are my socia[...]
imposed on [...]*

Is recogniti[...]

Preparing for Discussion

The Great Books program is based on shared
inquiry—the gradual unfolding of meaning that
occurs when readers explore a story or essay in
discussion. Shared inquiry cannot take place
unless all participants have immersed themselves
in the material and come to terms with it in their
various individual ways. This kind of involvement
teaches us to trust our own responses and to use
them as the basis for interpretation.

Discussion should be a free exchange of ideas
and a process of discovery. If you are seriously
attentive to a good story or essay, you will come
to discussion eager to share your ideas. During
discussion you will feel less concern about being
"right" or "wrong" than you will about increasing
your understanding of the material itself.

As part of your preparation for discussion,
read each selection at least twice, with a pen or
pencil in hand, and make notes of your thoughts
and feelings as you read. Your notes may take
any form you like: underline a passage, put a

question mark above a line, jot down a comment in the margin. If you are not allowed to mark your book, there are other ways to make notations: clip a note to an important page, use removable self-stick notes, or jot down your thoughts about a selection in a notebook reserved for the Great Books program. If you keep a special notebook, place a page number next to each note so that you can quickly refer to the passage on which the note is based.

On your first reading, make a note of what you don't understand, what seems important, and what you agree or disagree with. What you note, or the number of notes you make, doesn't matter; the very act of making notes will help you get involved with the material and begin thinking about it.

On a second reading you will find yourself making new notes, and probably more of them, simply because you have read the entire selection once before. New passages will strike you as important now that you know how the selection ends. You will discover connections between passages that you had missed on your first reading: the repetition of a significant word or phrase, a pattern of ideas or actions, or something in the beginning of a selection that prepares you for the ending. You may also begin to see how the different parts fit together and why the author uses certain phrases.

Having completed both readings, you should review your notes and try to turn some of them into questions that you would like the group's help in answering. It may be appropriate to raise these questions during discussion of the leader's questions, or the leader may set aside a separate time for them.

Here is an example of one reader's notes on the selection you have just read.

A man's *fame*, good or bad, and his _honor_ or dishonor <u>are names for one of his social selves.</u> The particular social self of a man called his honor is usually the result of one of those <u>splittings</u> of which we have spoken. It is his image in the eyes of his own "set," which exalts or condemns him as he conforms or not to certain <u>requirements</u> that may not be made of one in another walk of life. Thus a layman may abandon a city infected with cholera, but <u>a priest or a doctor would think such an act incompatible</u> with his honor. A soldier's honor requires him to fight or to die under circumstances where another man can apologize or run away with no stain upon his social self. A judge, a statesman, are in like manner debarred by the honor of their cloth from entering into pecuniary relations perfectly honorable to persons in private life. Nothing is commoner than to hear people discriminate between their <u>different selves</u> of this sort: "As a man I pity you, but as an official I must show you no mercy"; "As a politician I regard him as an ally, but <u>as a moralist I loathe him</u>"; etc., etc.

[Marginal notes:]

fame and honor as selves.

?

also incompatible with duty?

what about the instinct for self-preservation?

Is one of these selves the "real me"?

Is the moralist just one of my social selves?

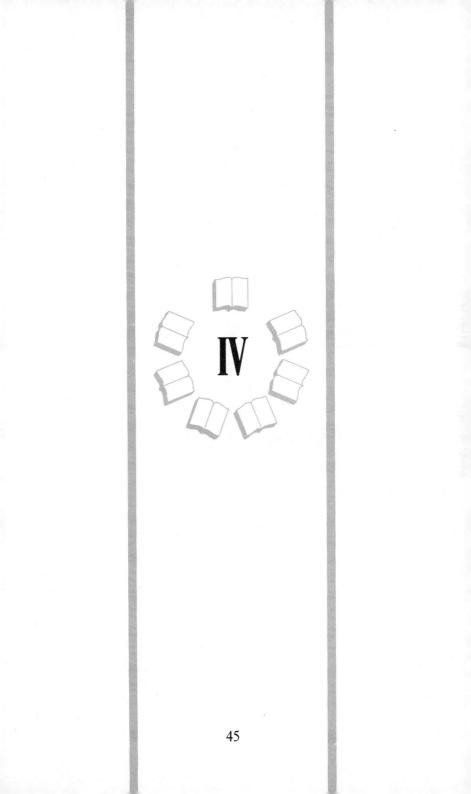

IV

What a Story Is

A famous writer once claimed that a novel should "hold a mirror up to the high road," catching and reflecting the passing scene just as it occurs. But even the most realistic fiction does something more interesting than this. Although a story may tell us a great deal about life at a given time and place, it is before all else a personal interpretation of experience. Thoughtful writers do not merely copy or imitate life, they shape it and endow it with meaning. As we read a story, we experience the world ordered by a particular intelligence and filtered through a particular sensibility. We see through the author's eyes. If we lend ourselves to the story fully, if we are seriously attentive, open, and alert, it may forever alter our own vision.

The best stories generally balance conflicting claims or points of view. As in life, situations in fiction are complex. Characters who are at odds with one another may both be right—or more likely, there will be right and wrong on both sides. Thoughtful stories present characters in the round, showing us more than we would know if we were in the story ourselves and more than we usually understand about the lives of those around us. By thinking about such stories, we come to see how each person has a distinct point of view—his or her own needs, desires, sorrows, and reasons for acting. We learn to look, in a conflict of interests, for the whole picture. Reading fiction not only broadens our sympathies for others but challenges us to re-examine ourselves, to move beyond our usual habits of perception and judgment.

Good stories require us to reach out to the author through active reading. As we read, it's important to ask ourselves what the author is trying to convey. What does he want us to think and feel? Why is he telling us this story? How does he feel about these characters? Does one character perhaps speak for the author?

Ultimately, readers must rely on their own responses to a story. A story then becomes a joint creation of the reader and the writer, a joint effort to make sense of life: a shared world created through words, to be imagined, explored, and interpreted. ▮▮

By and About Anton Chekhov

(1860–1904)

Anton Chekhov was born in Taganrog, a provincial port in southern Russia. He attended medical school at the University of Moscow, and after graduating, divided his time between medicine and writing. Looking back on his childhood, he once suggested it as material for a short story:

> Write a story, do, about a young man, the son of a serf, a former grocery boy, a choirsinger, a high school pupil and university student, brought up to respect rank, to kiss the hands of priests, to truckle to the ideas of others—a young man who expressed thanks for every piece of bread, who was whipped many times, who went without galoshes to do his tutoring, who used his fists, tortured animals, was fond of dining with rich relatives, was a hypocrite in his dealings with God and men, needlessly, solely out of a realization of his own insignificance—write how this young man squeezes the slave out of himself, drop by drop, and how, on awaking one fine morning, he feels that the blood coursing through his veins is no longer that of a slave but that of a real human being.

When criticized because his plays were not dramatic enough, he replied with a comment that also applies to his stories:

> In real life, people don't spend every minute shooting at each other, hanging themselves, and making confessions of love. They don't spend all the time saying clever things. They're more occupied with eating, drinking, flirting, and talking stupidities—and these are the things which ought to be shown on the stage. A play should be written in which people arrive, go away, have dinner, talk about the weather, and play cards. Life must be exactly as it is, and people as they are—not on stilts. . . . Let everything on the stage be just as complicated, and at the same time just as simple, as it is in life. People eat their dinner, just eat their dinner, and all the time their happiness is being established or their lives are being broken up.

His contemporary, Maxim Gorky, felt that no one understood the tragedy of life's trivialities as clearly and finely as Chekhov did. Gorky wrote:

> There passes before one a long file of men and women, slaves of their love, of their stupidity and idleness, of their greed for the good things of life; there walk the slaves of the dark fear of life; they struggle anxiously along, filling life with incoherent words about the future, feeling that in the present there is no place for them. . . .
>
> Many of them have nice dreams of how pleasant life will be in three hundred years, but it occurs to none of them to ask themselves who will make life pleasant if we only dream.
>
> In front of that dreary, gray crowd of helpless people there passed a great, wise, and observant man; he looked at all these dreary inhabitants of his country, and, with a sad smile, with a tone of gentle but deep reproach, with anguish in his face and in his heart, in a beautiful and sincere voice, he said to them:
>
> "You live badly, my friends. It is shameful to live like that."

Rothschild's Fiddle

Anton Chekhov

It was a small town, more wretched than a village, and almost all the inhabitants were old folk with a depressingly low death rate. Nor were many coffins required at the hospital and jail. In a word, business was bad. Had Jacob Ivanov been making coffins in a county town he would probably have owned a house and been called "mister." But in this dump he was plain Jacob, his street nickname was "Bronze" for whatever reason, and he lived as miserably as any farm laborer in his little old one-roomed shack which housed himself, his Martha, a stove, a double bed, coffins, his workbench and all his household goods.

Jacob made good solid coffins. For men—village and working-class folk—he made them to his own height, and never got them wrong because he was taller and stronger than anyone, even in the jail, though now seventy years old. For the gentry, though, and for women he made them to measure, using an iron ruler. He was not at all keen on orders for children's coffins, which he would knock up contemptuously without measuring. And when paid for them he would say that he "quite frankly set no store by such trifles."

His fiddle brought him a small income on top of his trade. A Jewish band usually played at weddings in the town, conducted by the tinker Moses Shakhkes who took more than half the proceeds. And since Jacob was a fine fiddler, especially with Russian folk tunes, Shakhkes sometimes asked him to join the band for fifty kopeks a day plus tips. Straightaway it made his face sweat and turn crimson, did sitting in the band. It was hot, there was a stifling smell of garlic, his fiddle squeaked. By his right ear wheezed the double-bass, by his left sobbed the flute played by a red-haired, emaciated Jew with a network of red and blue veins on his face. He was known as Rothschild after the noted millionaire. Now, this bloody little Jew even contrived to play the merriest tunes in lachrymose style. For no obvious reason Jacob became more and more obsessed by hatred and contempt for Jews, and for Rothschild in particular. He started picking on him and swearing at him. Once he made to beat him, whereat Rothschild took umbrage.

"I respect your talent, otherwise I am long ago throwing you out of window," he said with an enraged glare.

Then he burst into tears. This was why Bronze wasn't often asked to play in the band, but only in some dire crisis, when one of the Jews was unavailable.

Jacob was always in a bad mood because of the appalling waste of money he had to endure. For instance, it was a sin to work on a Sunday or a Saint's Day, while Mondays were unlucky, so that made two hundred odd days a year when you had to sit around idle. And that was all so much money wasted. If someone in town held a wedding without music, or Shakhkes didn't ask Jacob to play, that meant still more losses. The police superintendent had been ill for two years now. He was wasting away, and Jacob had waited impatiently for him to die, but the man had left for treatment in the county town, and damned if he didn't peg out there. Now, that was at least ten rubles down the drain, as his would have been an expensive coffin complete with brocade lining. Thoughts of these losses hounded Jacob mostly at night. He would put his fiddle on the bed beside him, and when some such tomfoolery preyed on his mind he would touch the strings and the fiddle would twang in the darkness. That made him feel better.

On the sixth of May in the previous year Martha had suddenly fallen ill. The old woman breathed heavily, drank a lot of water, was unsteady on her feet, but she would still do the stove herself of a morning, and even fetch the water. By evening, though, she would already be in bed. Jacob fiddled away all day. But when it was quite dark he took the book in which he listed his losses daily and began, out of sheer boredom, to add up the annual total. It came to more than a thousand rubles. This so shocked him that he flung his abacus on the floor and stamped his feet. Then he picked up the abacus and clicked away again for a while, sighing deep, heartfelt sighs. His face was purple and wet with sweat. He was thinking that if he had put that lost thousand in the bank he would have received at least forty rubles' interest a year. So that was forty more rubles down the drain. However hard you tried to wriggle out of it, everything was just a dead loss in fact.

Then he suddenly heard Martha call out. "Jacob, I'm dying."

He looked round at his wife. Her face was flushed in the heat, her expression was exceptionally bright and joyous. Accustomed to her pale face and timid, unhappy expression, Bronze was put out. She really did look as if she was dying, glad to be saying a permanent good-bye to hut, coffins and Jacob at long last.

Gazing at the ceiling and moving her lips, she looked happy, as if she could actually see her savior Death and was whispering to him.

It was dawn and the first rays were seen through the window. As he looked at the old woman, it vaguely occurred to Jacob that for some reason he had never shown her any affection all his life. Never had he been kind to her, never had he thought of buying her a kerchief or bringing her sweetmeats from a wedding. All he had done was yell at her, blame her for his "losses," threaten to punch her. True, he never had hit her. Still he had frightened her, she had always been petrified with fear. Yes, he had said she couldn't have tea because they had enough other expenses without that, so she only drank hot water. And now he knew why she looked so strangely joyous, and a chill went through him.

When it was fully light he borrowed a neighbor's horse and drove Martha to hospital. There were not many patients, so he did not have long to wait. Only about three hours. To his great joy the patients were not received on this occasion by the doctor, who was ill himself, but by his assistant Maxim, an old fellow said by everyone in town to be better than the doctor, drunken brawler though he was.

"I humbly greet you," said Jacob, taking his old woman into the consulting room. "You must excuse us troubling you with our trifling affairs, sir. Now, as you see, guv'nor, my old woman has fallen sick. She's my better half in a manner of speaking, if you'll pardon the expression——"

Frowning, stroking his side-whiskers, the white-eyebrowed assistant examined the old woman, who sat hunched on a stool, wizened, sharp-nosed, open-mouthed, her profile like a thirsty bird's.

"Hurrumph. Well, yes," the assistant slowly pronounced, and sighed. "It's influenza, fever perhaps. There's typhus in town. Ah well, the old woman's lived her life, praise the Lord. How old is she?"

"Seventy come next year, guv'nor."

"Ah well, her life's over. Time she was on her way."

"It's true enough, what you just said, sir." Jacob smiled out of politeness. "And we thanks you most kindly for being so nice about it, like. But, if you'll pardon the expression, every insect wants to live."

"Not half it does." The assistant's tone suggested that it depended on him whether the old woman lived or died. "Now then, my good man, you put a cold compress on her head and give her one of these powders twice a day. And now cheerio to you. A very bong jour."

From his face Jacob could tell that it was all up, and that no powders would help now. Obviously Martha was going to die soon, either today or tomorrow. He gave the assistant's elbow a push and winked.

"We ought to cup her, Mr. Maxim sir," he said in a low voice.

"Haven't the time, my good man. Take your old woman and be off with you. So long and all that."

"Begging your kindness, sir," implored Jacob. "As you know, mister, if it was her guts or her innards, like, what was sick, then it's powders and drops she should have. But this here is a chill, and the great thing with chills is to bleed 'em, sir."

But the assistant had already called for his next patient, and a village woman with a little boy had come into the consulting room.

"Buzz off you, beat it!" The assistant frowned at Jacob. "Don't hang around."

"Then at least put some leeches to her. I'll be grateful to you all my life, I will."

The assistant lost his temper.

"Don't you bandy words with me," he yelled. "D-damned oaf!"

Jacob lost his temper too, and turned completely crimson. But he grabbed Martha's arm without a single word and took her out of the room. Only when they were getting into their cart did he cast a stern, mocking look at that hospital.

"They're a high and mighty lot round here," he said. "He'd have cupped a rich man, I'll be bound, but for a poor one he grudges even a single leech. Bastards!"

They arrived home, and Martha, after entering the house, stood for about ten minutes gripping the stove. If she was to lie down Jacob would talk about all the money he'd lost and blame her for lolling about and not wanting to work—or so she thought. And Jacob looked at her miserably, remembering that tomorrow was St. John's Day, and the day after that was St. Nicholas's Day, after which came Sunday and Unlucky Monday. That made four days when he couldn't work. But Martha was sure to die on one of those days, so he must make the coffin today. He took his iron ruler, went up to the old woman and measured her. Then she lay down and he crossed himself and started on the coffin.

When the work was finished, Jacob put on his spectacles and wrote in his book.

"Martha Ivanov: to one coffin, 2 rubles 40 kopeks."

He sighed. The old woman lay there all the time silently, her eyes shut, but when it grew dark that evening she suddenly called the old man.

"Remember fifty years ago, Jacob?" She looked at him happily. "God gave us a little fair-haired baby, remember? We were always sitting by the river, you and I, singing songs under the willow tree." She laughed bitterly. "The little girl died."

Jacob cudgeled his brains, but could recall neither baby nor willow. "You're imagining things."

The priest came and gave the last rites, whereupon Martha mumbled something or other. By morning she was gone.

Old women neighbors washed her, dressed her, laid her in her coffin. So as not to waste money on the sexton, Jacob read the lesson himself, and he got the grave for nothing because the cemetery caretaker was a crony of his. Four peasants bore the coffin to the cemetery out of respect, not for money. It was followed by old women, beggars and two village idiots while people in the street crossed themselves piously. Jacob was delighted that it was all so right and seemly, that it didn't cost much or hurt anyone's feelings. As he said good-bye to Martha for the last time he touched the coffin.

"Good workmanship, that," he thought.

But on his way back from the cemetery he was overcome by a great sorrow. He felt vaguely unwell. His breath came hot and heavy, his legs were weak, he felt thirsty. Then various thoughts began to prey on his mind. He again remembered that never in his life had he been kind to Martha or shown her affection. The fifty-two years of their life together in one hut—it seemed such a long, long time. But somehow he had never given her a thought in all that time, he had no more noticed her than a cat or dog. But she had made up the stove every day, hadn't she? She had cooked, baked, fetched water, cut wood, shared his bed. And when he came back from weddings drunk she would reverently hang his fiddle on the wall and put him to bed—all this in silence, looking scared and troubled.

Rothschild approached Jacob, smiling and bowing.

"I been looking for you, mister," he said. "Mister Moses sends his respects, says he vonts you at once."

Jacob wasn't interested. He wanted to cry.

"Leave me alone." He walked on.

"Vot are you doing?" Rothschild ran ahead, much alarmed. "Mister Moses'll be offended. You're to come at once, said he."

Out of breath, blinking, with all those red freckles, the Jew disgusted Jacob. The green frock coat with the black patches, his whole frail, puny figure—what a loathsome sight.

"Keep out of my way, Garlic-breath," shouted Jacob. "You leave me alone."

The Jew, angered, also shouted. "You are being quiet please or I am throwing you over fence."

"Out of my sight, you!" bellowed Jacob, pouncing on him with clenched fists. "Proper poison, them greasy bastards are."

Scared to death, Rothschild crouched down, waving his hands above his head as if warding off blows, then jumped up and scampered off as fast as he could, hopping about and flapping his arms as he ran. You could see the quaking of his long, thin back. At this the street urchins gleefully rushed after him shouting "Dirty Yid!" Barking dogs chased him too. Someone roared with laughter and then whistled, the dogs barked louder and in closer harmony.

Then a dog must have bitten Rothschild, for a shout of pain and despair was heard.

Jacob walked on the common, then started off along the edge of the town without knowing where he was going. "There's old Jake, there he goes," shouted the boys. Then he came to the river. Here sandpipers swooped and twittered, ducks quacked. The sun's heat beat down and the water sparkled till it hurt the eyes. Walking along the towpath, Jacob saw a buxom, red-cheeked woman emerge from a bathing hut.

"Damn performing seal," he thought.

Not far from the bathing hut boys were fishing for crayfish, using meat as bait. They saw him.

"Hey, there's old Jake," they shouted nastily.

Then came the broad old willow tree with its huge hollow and crows' nests.

Suddenly Jacob's memory threw up a vivid image of that

fair-haired baby and the willow that Martha had spoken of. Yes, it was the same willow—so green, so quiet, so sad.

How old it had grown, poor thing.

He sat beneath it and began remembering. On the other bank, now a water meadow, had been a silver-birch forest, and over there on that bare hill on the horizon the dark blue bulk of an ancient pine wood. Barges had plied up and down the river. But now it was all flat and bare with the one little silver birch on the near side, slim and youthful as a young girl. There were only ducks and geese on the river, and it was hard to think that barges had ever passed here. Even the geese seemed fewer. Jacob shut his eyes and pictured vast flocks of white geese swooping towards each other.

How was it, he wondered, that he had never been by the river in the last forty or fifty years of his life. Or, if he had, it had made no impression on him. Why, this was a proper river, not just any old stream. You could fish it, you could sell the fish to shopkeepers, clerks and the man who kept the station bar, you could put the money in the bank. You could sail a boat from one riverside estate to another playing your fiddle, and all manner of folk would pay you for it. You could try starting up the barges again—better than making coffins, that was. Then you could breed geese, slaughter them and send them to Moscow in winter. "The down alone would fetch ten rubles a year, I'll be bound." But he had let all this go by, he had done nothing about it. Oh, what a waste, what a waste of money! If you put it all together—fishing, fiddling, barging, goose-slaughtering—what a lot of money you'd have made. But none of it had happened, not even in your dreams. Life had flowed past without profit, without enjoyment—gone aimlessly, leaving nothing to show for it. The future was empty. And if you looked back there was only all the awful waste of money that sent shivers down your spine. Why couldn't a man live without all that loss and waste? And why, he wondered, had they cut down the birch forest? And the pine wood? Why wasn't that common put to use? Why do people always do the wrong things? Why had Jacob spent all his life cursing, bellowing, threatening people with his fists, ill-treating his wife? And what, oh what, was the point of scaring and insulting that Jew just now? Why are people generally such a nuisance to each other? After all, it's all such a waste of money, a terrible waste it is. Without the hate and malice folks could get a lot of profit out of each other.

That evening and night he had visions of baby, willow, fish, dead geese, of Martha with her thirsty bird's profile, and of Rothschild's wretched, pale face, while various other gargoyle-like faces advanced on him from all sides muttering about all the waste of money. He tossed and turned, he got out of bed half a dozen times to play his fiddle.

Next morning he forced himself to get up and went to the hospital. That same Maxim told him to put a cold compress on his head and gave him powders, but his look and tone made Jacob realize that it was all up and that no powders would help now. Later, on his way home, he reckoned that death would be pure gain to him. He wouldn't have to eat, drink, pay taxes or offend folk. And since a man lies in his grave not just one but hundreds and thousands of years, the profit would be colossal. Man's life is debit, his death credit. The argument was correct, of course, but painfully disagreeable too. Why are things so oddly arranged? You only live once, so why don't you get anything out of it?

He didn't mind dying, but when he got home and saw his fiddle his heart missed a beat and he felt sorry. He couldn't take his fiddle with him to the grave, so it would be orphaned and go the way of the birches and the pines. Nothing in this world has ever come to anything, nothing ever will. Jacob went out of the hut and sat in the doorway clasping the fiddle to his breast. Thinking of his wasted, profitless life, he started playing he knew not what, but it came out poignantly moving and tears coursed down his cheeks. The harder he thought the sadder grew the fiddle's song.

The latch squeaked twice and Rothschild appeared at the garden gate. He crossed half the yard boldly, but when he saw Jacob he suddenly stopped, cringed and—through fear, no doubt—gesticulated as if trying to indicate the time with his fingers.

"Come along then," said Jacob kindly, beckoning him. "It's all right."

Looking at him mistrustfully and fearfully, Rothschild began to approach but stopped a few feet away.

"Don't hit me, I beg you." He squatted down. "It's Mister Moses has sent me again. Never fear, says he, you go to Jacob again—tell him we can't do without him, he says. There's a vedding on Vednesday. Aye, that there is. Mister Shapovalov is marrying his daughter to a fine young man. A rich folks' vedding this, and no mistake!" The Jew screwed up one eye.

"Can't be done." Jacob breathed heavily. "I'm ill, son."

He again struck up, his tears spurting on to the fiddle. Rothschild listened carefully, standing sideways on, arms crossed on his breast. His scared, baffled look gradually gave way to a sorrowful, suffering expression. He rolled his eyes as if in anguished delight.

"A-a-ah!" he said as the tears crawled down his cheeks and splashed on his green frock coat.

After that Jacob lay down all day, sick at heart. When the priest heard his confession that evening and asked whether he remembered committing any particular sin he exerted his failing memory and once more recalled Martha's unhappy face and the desperate yell of the Jew bitten by a dog.

"Give my fiddle to Rothschild," he said in a voice barely audible.

"Very well," the priest answered.

Now everyone in town wants to know where Rothschild got such a fine fiddle. Did he buy it, did he steal it? Or did someone leave it with him as a pledge? He only plays the fiddle now, having given up the flute long ago. From his bow there flow those same poignant strains which used to come from his flute. But when he tries to repeat the tune Jacob had played in his doorway the outcome is so sad and mournful that his listeners weep and he ends by rolling his eyes up with an "A-a-ah!"

So popular is this new tune in town that merchants and officials are always asking Rothschild over and making him play it a dozen times.

Interpretive Questions

1. Why does Jacob think of life as a debit and death as a credit?

2. Why doesn't Jacob remember his daughter?

3. Why does Jacob think of his fiddle as an orphan?

4. Why does Jacob leave his fiddle to Rothschild?

5. Why is it made a mystery to the townspeople how Rothschild got his fiddle?

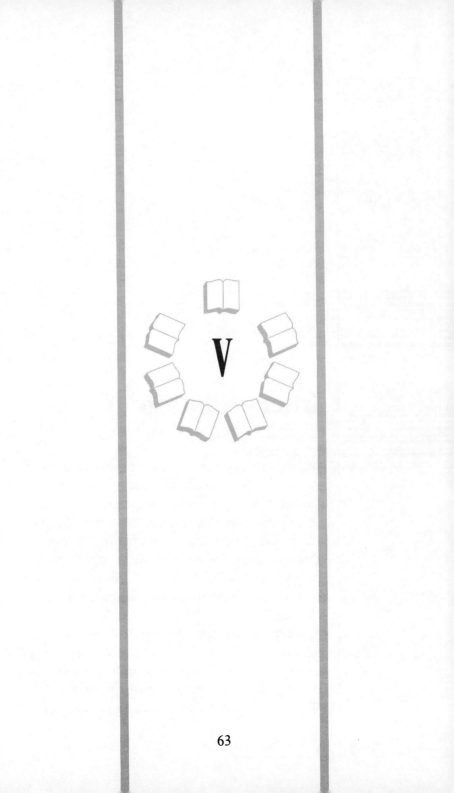

V

Interpretation

Interpretation is the effort we make to understand
what we read—to explain what an author's
language is designed to make us think or feel.
Interpreting the selections in this series requires
effort because they have been written by keen
thinkers. What these authors have to say cannot
be taken in hastily. They use words carefully and
precisely, but sometimes their language is
difficult.

We begin to interpret a selection the first time
we read it. It is helpful to make notes on what we
understand and what puzzles us during this
reading. Reading slowly is also important.
Whenever you don't understand a passage, try

pausing and rereading it. If an unfamiliar word stops you, look it up in a dictionary. If the author has used an ordinary word in an unfamiliar way, try to figure out its meaning in the context of the words or sentences surrounding it. If the passage is still unclear, make a note of it and move on; the meaning may be clarified later in the selection.

By the end of your first reading you may have only a glimmer of the selection's meaning, but your bits and pieces of understanding will help you on a second reading. This time you will be able to think about the selection as a whole, not just about the next step in an argument or how a story will end. You will be in a better position to consider why an author made a particular statement, why it was phrased in a certain way, and why it appears where it does in the selection. You should at least be able to pinpoint why you don't understand what the author is saying. During this reading, make a note of connections you find between different parts of the selection. Check the meaning of what you think you understand by expressing it in your own words.

Discussion is the last step in the interpretive process. It is an opportunity to compare your understanding of a selection's meaning with the interpretations of others, to discover significant passages that you may have overlooked, and to hear explanations of what you didn't understand. Occasionally discussion may provide your first inkling about a selection's meaning, but more often it explores ideas you had while reading. ∎∎

By and About Adam Smith

(1723–1790)

Adam Smith was neither a businessman nor a high-ranking government official nor, strictly speaking, an economist. He was a professor of moral philosophy. That discipline included economics, political science, ethics, and sociology, all of which are discussed in *The Wealth of Nations.*

On consumer demand:

> The desire of food is limited in every man by the narrow capacity of the human stomach, but the desire of the conveniences and ornaments of building, dress, equipage, and household furniture seems to have no limit or certain boundary.

On the extravagance of government:

> It is the highest impertinence and presumption . . . in kings and ministers, to pretend to watch over the economy of private people. . . . They are themselves always, and without exception, the greatest spendthrifts in the society. If their own extravagance does not ruin the state, that of their subjects never will.

On the use of force by government:

> For though management and persuasion are always the easiest and the safest instruments of governments, as force and violence are the worst and the most dangerous, yet such, it seems, is the natural insolence of man that he almost always disdains to use the good instrument, except when he cannot or dare not use the bad one.

On invention:

> In the first fire-engines, a boy was constantly employed to open and shut alternately the communication between the boiler and the cylinder, according as the piston either ascended or descended. One of those boys, who loved to play with his companions, observed that by tying a string from the handle of the valve which opened this communication to another part of the machine, the valve would open and shut without his assistance and

leave him at liberty to divert himself with his playfellows. One of the greatest improvements that has been made upon this machine, since it was first invented, was in this manner the discovery of a boy who wanted to save his own labor.

On trade associations:

People of the same trade seldom meet together, even for merriment and diversion, but the conversation ends in a conspiracy against the public, or in some contrivance to raise prices.

According to Smith, the wealth of a nation consists not in its supply of gold and silver, but in its annual production of goods and services. This wealth increases dramatically when members of a society begin to specialize in the goods they produce and the services they render: a specialized laborer is more efficient and productive than a nonspecialist and thus increases personal income while adding to the national wealth. An enlightened society therefore allows individuals to pursue their chosen specialties. Smith is confident that individuals seeking only their own advantage will be led by an "invisible hand" to further (unknowingly) the good of society. In our selection, Smith explains how the division of labor springs from the human desire for self-betterment. Does Smith's further claim, that we can count more on our neighbor's desire for self-betterment than on his benevolence, imply a bleak view of human nature?

Concerning the Division of Labor

Adam Smith

This division of labor, from which so many advantages are derived, is not originally the effect of any human wisdom, which foresees and intends that general opulence to which it gives occasion. It is the necessary, though very slow and gradual, consequence of a certain propensity in human nature which has in view no such extensive utility; the propensity to truck, barter, and exchange one thing for another.

Whether this propensity be one of those original principles in human nature, of which no further account can be given; or whether, as seems more probable, it be the necessary consequence of the faculties of reason and speech, it belongs not to our present subject to enquire. It is common to all men, and to be found in no other race of animals, which seem to know neither this nor any other species of contracts. Two greyhounds, in running down the same hare, have sometimes the appearance of acting in some sort of concert. Each turns her

---

*A selection from *The Wealth of Nations*.

towards his companion, or endeavors to intercept her when his companion turns her towards himself. This, however, is not the effect of any contract, but of the accidental concurrence of their passions in the same object at that particular time. Nobody ever saw a dog make a fair and deliberate exchange of one bone for another with another dog. Nobody ever saw one animal by its gestures and natural cries signify to another, this is mine, that yours; I am willing to give this for that. When an animal wants to obtain something either of a man or of another animal, it has no other means of persuasion but to gain the favor of those whose service it requires. A puppy fawns upon its dam, and a spaniel endeavors by a thousand attractions to engage the attention of its master who is at dinner, when it wants to be fed by him. Man sometimes uses the same arts with his brethren, and when he has no other means of engaging them to act according to his inclinations, endeavors by every servile and fawning attention to obtain their good will. He has not time, however, to do this upon every occasion. In civilized society he stands at all times in need of the cooperation and assistance of great multitudes, while his whole life is scarce sufficient to gain the friendship of a few persons. In almost every other race of animals each individual, when it is grown up to maturity, is entirely independent, and in its natural state has occasion for the assistance of no other living creature. But man has almost constant occasion for the help of his brethren, and it is in vain for him to expect it from their benevolence only. He will be more likely to prevail if he can interest their self-love in his favor, and show them that it is for their own advantage to do for him what he requires of them. Whoever offers to another a bargain of any kind, proposes to do this. Give me that which I want, and you shall have this which you want, is the meaning of every such offer; and it is in this manner that we obtain from one another the far greater part of those good offices which we stand in need of. It is not from the benevolence of the butcher, the brewer, or the baker that we expect our dinner, but from their regard to their own interest. We address ourselves, not to their humanity but to their self-love, and never talk to them of our own necessities but of their advantages. Nobody but a beggar chooses to depend chiefly upon the benevolence of his fellow citizens. Even a beggar does not depend upon it entirely. The charity of well-disposed people, indeed, supplies him with the whole fund of his subsistence. But though this principle ultimately provides him with all the necessaries of life which he has occasion for, it neither does nor can provide him with them as he has occasion for them. The greater part of his occasional wants are supplied in the same manner as those of other people, by treaty, by barter, and by purchase. With the money which one man gives him he purchases food. The old clothes which another bestows upon him he exchanges for other old clothes which suit him better, or for lodging, or for food, or for money, with which he can buy either food, clothes, or lodging, as he has occasion.

As it is by treaty, by barter, and by purchase that we obtain from one another the greater part of those mutual good offices which we stand in need of, so it is this same trucking disposition which originally gives occasion to the division of labor. In a tribe of hunters or shepherds a particular person makes bows and arrows, for example, with more readiness and dexterity than any other. He frequently exchanges them for cattle or for venison with his companions, and he finds at last that he can in this manner get more cattle and venison than if he himself went to the field to catch them. From a regard to his own interest, therefore, the making of bows and arrows grows to be his chief business, and he becomes a sort of armorer. Another excels in making the frames and covers of their little huts or movable houses. He is accustomed to be of use in this way to his neighbors, who reward him in the same manner with cattle and with venison, till at last he finds it his interest to dedicate himself entirely to this employment and to become a sort of house carpenter. In the same manner a third becomes a smith or a brazier; a fourth a tanner or dresser of hides or skins, the principal part of the clothing of savages. And thus the certainty of being able to exchange all that surplus part of the produce of his own labor, which is over and above his own consumption, for such parts of the produce of other men's labor as he may have occasion for, encourages every man to apply himself to a particular occupation, and to cultivate and bring to perfection whatever talent or genius he may possess for that particular species of business.

The difference of natural talents in different men is, in reality, much less than we are aware of; and the very different genius which appears to distinguish men of different professions, when grown up to maturity, is not upon many occasions so much the cause as the effect of the division of labor. The difference between the most dissimilar characters, between a philosopher and a common street porter, for example, seems to arise not so much from nature as from habit, custom, and education. When they came into the world, and for the first six or eight years of their existence, they were, perhaps, very much alike, and neither their parents nor playfellows could perceive any remarkable difference. About that age, or soon after, they come to be employed in very different occupations. The difference of talents comes then to be taken notice of, and widens by degrees, till at last the vanity of the philosopher is willing to acknowledge scarce any resemblance. But without the disposition to truck, barter, and exchange, every man must have procured to himself every necessary and conveniency of life which he wanted. All must have had the same duties to perform, and the same work to do, and there could have been no such difference of employment as could alone give occasion to any great difference of talents.

As it is this disposition which forms that difference of talents, so remarkable among men of different professions, so it is this same disposition which renders that difference useful. Many tribes of animals acknowledged to be all of the same species, derive from nature a much more remarkable distinction of genius than what, antecedent to custom and education, appears to take place among men. By nature a philosopher is not in genius and disposition half so different from a street porter, as a mastiff is from a greyhound, or a greyhound from a spaniel, or this last from a shepherd's dog. Those different tribes of animals, however, though all of the same species, are of scarce any use to one another. The strength of the mastiff is not in the least supported either by the swiftness of the greyhound, or by the sagacity of the spaniel, or by the docility of the shepherd's dog. The effects of those different geniuses and talents, for want of the power or disposition to barter and exchange, cannot be brought into a common stock, and do not in the least contribute to the better accommodation and conveniency of the species. Each animal is still obliged to support and defend itself, separately and independently, and derives no sort of advantage from that variety of talents with which nature has distinguished its fellows. Among men, on the contrary, the most dissimilar geniuses are of use to one another; the different produces of their respective talents, by the general disposition to truck, barter, and exchange, being brought, as it were, into a common stock, where every man may purchase whatever part of the produce of other men's talents he has occasion for.

Interpretive Questions

1. Why, according to Smith, is self-love more likely to perpetuate a civilized society than benevolence is?

2. Does Smith have a low opinion of human nature?

3. Why does Smith emphasize that differences in talent are more the effect than the cause of the division of labor?

4. Does Smith assume that all people can recognize and pursue their own self-interest?

5. Why does Smith want to establish that the propensity to truck, barter, and exchange is natural, while differences in talent are not?

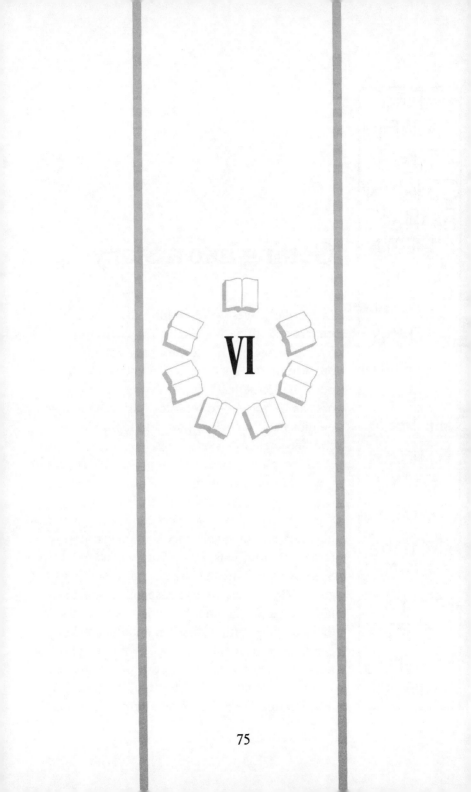

VI

Getting Into a Story

In our daily lives we often have to act before we understand; there is seldom time for simply feeling or seeing. But a story provides an opportunity for such reflection and a release from our usual responsibilities. It invites us to step outside ourselves—to set aside our prejudices and opinions and see what the world looks like from another angle of vision.

As we read a story, we observe the characters in their most private moments. We eavesdrop on their conversations and learn their innermost thoughts. Yet they pay us no mind, and no matter how intense our involvement, we never quite forget that they exist in a realm beyond our help. Since we stand neither to gain nor to lose by what goes on in a story, we can suspend judgment in favor of understanding. Reading a story is a way to participate, without risk, in another world.

Before we can enter the world of a story, we must first bring it to life in our minds. Envisioning a story—recreating an author's world in our own imagination—begins with an alertness to details and a sensuous or artistic appreciation of them. The details of a story guide reflection, anchoring our thoughts and feelings. They also serve, with our assistance, to bring characters and scenes to life.

Since writers seldom spell everything out for their readers, getting into a story involves not only collecting details, but a process of inference as well. For example, it would be a pointless exercise for even a very talented writer to attempt to describe a character completely. What he does instead is give us the most revealing or meaningful details. In fiction, the salient features of a face are apt to correspond to a character's inner world or to suggest something of his meaning for an author. With repetition and emphasis, physical facts may take on symbolic value.

In the best stories, each detail is carefully chosen not only for its power to evoke reality, but also as a guide to meaningful reflection. Our first priority, then, is to gather the "sunny trifles" of the story—to savor its concrete details. Through them the world of the story comes into being: the atmosphere builds and the shadowy figures of the author's imagination take on flesh. If these characters and their world possess what a poet called a "semblance of truth and sufficient human interest," they win our credence, or a "willing suspension of disbelief for the moment." Then we cease to be aware of the effort we are expending as we read. Our curiosity carries us through the story, which we read with passion and understanding. ∎

By and About Maxim Gorky

(1868–1936)

Gorky, "the bitter," is the pen name of Alexy Maximovich Peshkov. A friend of Tolstoy and Chekhov, as well as of Lenin, Gorky stands between the Russia of the tsars and the Soviet Union. Rebellion is the recurrent theme of his life. He never betrayed his youthful boast: "I have come into this world so as to disagree."

After he was orphaned at ten, Gorky found work as an assistant in a shoe shop, a rag-and-bone collector, dishwasher on a Volga steamboat, apprentice icon painter, and even bird catcher. In his autobiography, he describes the strange outcasts he encountered in his wanderings through Russia:

> To ward off starvation I used to go down to the wharves along the Volga, where it was easy to earn fifteen or twenty kopeks. Surrounded by stevedores, tramps, and thieves, I felt just like a piece of iron thrown onto a heap of red-hot coal, and every day filled me with countless impressions that were painful and not easily forgotten. Those men there, with their naked greed and crude instincts, spun before me like a whirlwind, and their angry feelings toward life, their derisively hostile attitude towards the whole world, their indifference to what happened to themselves, drew me towards them and made me want to plunge myself into the same cynical world. . . . Sometimes, on stifling nights, men would cross the river Kazanka to the meadows and lie among the bushes, drinking, eating, chatting about their personal affairs, but more often about the complexities of life, about the strange muddle of human relationships.

At about the age of twenty, Gorky became aware of his vocation:

> I realized that I had seen, heard, and lived through much that people could and should be told of. It seemed to me that I knew and felt certain things differently from the way other people did; this both perturbed me and put me in an unquiet and talkative

frame of mind. . . . I often felt intoxicated and experienced attacks of volubility, and a gush of words, from an urge to give expression to all that oppressed or gladdened me; I was eager to "get things off my chest."

Looking back on this period in his life, he recalled the decisive influence of books:

Books whispered in my ear of the existence of another life, one that was more worthy of man than that which I was living. . . . They showed me my place in life. . . . Books bred in me a sense of personal responsibility for all the evil in life and evoked in me a reverence for the human mind's creativity.

It is with profound belief in the truth of my conviction that I say to all: Love books; they will make your life easier, render you friendly service in finding your way through the motley and tumultuous confusion of ideas, emotions, and happenings, teach you to respect yourself and others, and fill the mind and the heart with love for the world and man.

Even if hostile to your beliefs, any book that has been written in honesty, out of love of people, out of good will, is admirable.

Chelkash

Maxim Gorky

I

The blue southern sky was so obscured by dust that it had a murky look. The hot sun stared down at the greenish sea as through a thin gray veil, and its rays found poor reflection in the water, churned up as it was by the strokes of oars, the propellers of steamers, and the sharp keels of Turkish feluccas and other craft which ploughed the crowded harbor in all directions. The waves of the sea, crushed within their granite encasements by the enormous weights gliding over their surfaces, hurled themselves at the shore and the sides of the ships—hurled themselves growling and foaming, their flanks littered with all sorts of rubbish.

The clang of anchor chains, the clash of the buffers of goods cars, the metallic wail of sheets of iron being unloaded on to paving stones, the dull thump of wood against wood, the clatter of carts, the whistle of steamships rising from a wail to a shriek, the shouts of stevedores, seamen, and customs guards—

all this merged to form the deafening music of the working day which surged rebelliously in the sky above the harbor, while from the earth below new waves of sound kept rising to meet it—now a rumble that shook the earth, now a crash that rent the sultry air.

The granite, the steel, the wood, the paving stones, the ships, and the people—everything was impregnated with the mighty sounds of this impassioned hymn to Mercury.* But human voices could hardly be detected in the general chorus, so weak and even ridiculous were they. And the people themselves, they whose efforts had given birth to all this sound, were ridiculous and pitiable; their ragged dirty wiry bodies were bent double under the loads on their backs as they rushed hither and thither in the dust and the heat and the noise, and they were as nothing compared with the steel leviathans, the mountains of merchandise, and clanging railway cars, and all the other things which they themselves had created. The things of their own creating had enslaved them and robbed them of personality.

The gigantic ships lying with steam up whistled and hissed and heaved great sighs, and every sound they uttered was filled with mocking contempt for the drab and dusty creatures crawling over their decks to load their deep holds with the products of the servile labor. It made one laugh till the tears ran to see these long files of stevedores carrying thousands of poods† of grain on their backs to be deposited in the iron bellies of the ships so that they themselves might earn a few pounds of grain to fill their own bellies. A poem of bitter irony could be read in the contrast between these ragged sweating men, stupefied

* *Mercury.* The Roman god of commerce.
† A *pood* equals 36 pounds.

by the heat, the noise, and the exhausting labor, and the powerful machines these men had made and which stood radiating well-being in the sunlight—machines which, when all is said and done, had been set in motion not by steam, but by the blood and muscles of those who made them.

The noise was oppressive; the dust tickled the nose and got into the eyes; the heat scorched and enervated the body; and everything seemed tense, as if the end of endurance had been reached and catastrophe was imminent, a tremendous explosion that would clear the air so that men might breathe freely and easily. And then silence would descend on the world and there would be no more dust and turmoil to deafen and irritate people and drive them mad; and the air of the town, of the sea, and of the sky would be fresh and clear and beautiful. . . .

Twelve measured strokes of a bell were heard. When the last brassy vibrations had died away the savage music of labor was found to have subsided, and a minute later it turned into a mere rumble of discontent. Now the voices of the people and the plash of the sea were more audible. It was the dinner hour.

II

When the stevedores stopped work and scattered over the docks in noisy groups to buy victuals from the vendors and find shady corners where they could squat on the pavement to take their meal, Grishka Chelkash put in an appearance. He was well known to all the dockers, a confirmed drunkard, a bold and clever thief. He was barefooted and bareheaded, had on a pair of threadbare corduroy trousers and a filthy cotton shirt with a torn collar that exposed a bony chest covered by brown skin. The matted state of his iron-gray hair and the crumpled look of his lean and hawk-like face indicated that he had just waked up. A straw had become caught in his moustache, another in the stubble of his left cheek, while behind his ear he had stuck a sprig of linden. Long and lanky and a bit stooped, he sauntered slowly down the cobbled street, sniffing the air with his hooked nose and casting a glittering gray eye about him as he searched for someone among the dockers. His long dark moustache kept twitching like a cat's; he held his hands behind his back and kept rubbing them together and twisting his crooked grasping fingers. Even here, among hundreds of other roughs, he instantly attracted attention because of the resemblance to a steppe-hawk conveyed by his predatory leanness and aimful walk, which, like the flight of the bird of prey he resembled, concealed a tense alertness under an appearance of poised tranquillity.

As he came up to a group of stevedores sitting in the shadow cast by a pile of coal baskets, a stocky young chap, with a blotched and vapid face and with scratches on his neck suggesting a recent fight, got up to meet him. He fell into step beside Chelkash and said under his breath:

"The seamen have discovered two bales of cloth missing. They're searching."

"So what?" Chelkash asked, calmly running his eyes over him.

"What d'ye mean 'so what'? They're searching, I tell you."

"And you thought I might join in the search?"

"Go to hell!"

The chap turned back.

"Wait! Who gave you those beauty marks? A pity to mess up your shop front like that! Seen Mishka?"

"Not for a long time," called back the chap as he joined his comrades.

Everybody who met Chelkash greeted him as an old acquaintance, but he, usually so cheery and biting, must have been out of sorts, for his replies were all very terse.

From behind a pile of merchandise suddenly appeared a

customs guard—dark-green, dusty, aggressively erect. He planted himself in front of Chelkash in a challenging pose, his left hand on the hilt of his dirk, his right reaching out for Chelkash's collar.

"Halt! Where you bound?"

Chelkash retreated a step, lifted his eyes to the guard's red face and gave a cool smile.

The face, wily but good-natured, tried to assume a dread aspect: the cheeks puffed out and turned purple, the brows drew together, the eyes rolled, and the effect on the whole was extremely comical.

"I told you once to keep away from these docks if you didn't want me to smash your ribs in, and here you are again!" he roared.

"Howdy, Semyonich! Haven't seen you for a long time," said the imperturbable Chelkash, holding out his hand.

"I wouldn't cry if I didn't see you for another fifty years. Move on, move on."

But he shook the extended hand.

"Here's what I wanted to ask," went on Chelkash, holding the guard's hand in steel fingers and shaking it in an intimate sort of way. "Seen Mishka anywhere?"

"What Mishka? I don't know any Mishka. Move on, man, or the packhouse guard may see you and then——"

"The red-headed chap I worked with on the *Kostroma* last time," persisted Chelkash.

"That you *thieved* with, you mean. They've put him in hospital, that Mishka of yours—got his leg crushed by some iron. Get out of here, I tell you, get out before I throw you out by the scruff of the neck."

"Listen to that, now! And you said you didn't know no Mishka. What makes you so nasty, Semyonich?"

"None of your talk! Get out!"

The guard was getting angry; he glanced about him and tried to free his hand, but Chelkash held on to it as he looked at him calmly from under bushy eyebrows and went on talking:

"What's the rush? Don't you want to have a nice little chat with me? How you getting on? How's the wife and kiddies? Well?" His eyes twinkled and his teeth flashed in a mocking grin as he added: "Been wanting to drop in to see you for ever so long, but just can't seem to manage it. It's the drink——"

"Drop it, I tell you! None of your joking, you lanky lubber. I mean what I say. But maybe you're turning to house-breaking, or robbing people in the street?"

"Why should I? There's enough here to keep you and me busy a lifetime. Honest there is, Semyonich. But I hear you've snitched another two bales of cloth. Watch out, or you'll find yourself in trouble yet!"

Semyonich trembled with indignation and the saliva flew as he tried to give voice to it. Chelkash let go of his hand and calmly strode off on his long legs to the dock gates. The guard followed at his heels, cursing him roundly.

Chelkash was in better spirits now; he whistled a tune through his teeth, thrust his hands into his pockets, and retarded his steps, tossing off well-aimed quips to right and left. He was paid in his own coin.

"Just see what good care of you the bosses are taking, Grishka!" called out a stevedore who was stretched out on the ground with his comrades, taking a rest after their meal.

"Semyonich's seeing I don't step on any nails in my bare feet," replied Chelkash.

They got to the gates. Two soldiers ran their hands down Chelkash's clothes and pushed him out into the street.

He crossed the road and sat down on the curbstone opposite a pub. A line of loaded carts came thundering out of the dock gates, while a line of empty ones moved in the other direction, their drivers bouncing in their seats. The docks belched forth a roar of sound and clouds of dust that stuck to the skin.

Chelkash was in his element amid this mad welter. He was anticipating a good haul that night, a haul that would cost him little effort but require a great deal of skill. He did not doubt but that his skill was sufficient, and he screwed up his eyes with pleasure as he reflected on how he would spend all his bank notes the next morning. He thought of his pal Mishka. He needed him badly, and here he had gone and broken his leg. Chelkash cursed under his breath, for he feared he could not handle the job alone. What would the weather be like? He glanced up at the sky, then down the street.

Sitting on the pavement, his back against a hitching post some half a dozen paces away, was a young lad in a blue homespun shirt and trousers, with bast sandals on his feet and a torn brown cap on his head. Beside him lay a small knapsack and a haftless scythe wrapped in straw and neatly tied with string. The lad was sturdy, broad-shouldered, fair-haired, his face was tanned by wind and sun, and he had large blue eyes that stared amiably at Chelkash.

Chelkash bared his teeth, stuck out his tongue, made a frightful face and stared back with popping eyes.

The boy blinked in astonishment at first, then he burst out laughing, calling out between spasms: "Crazy as a loon!" Without getting up, he hitched along the curbstone to where Chelkash was sitting, dragging his knapsack through the dust and allowing the tip of his scythe to clank over the cobbles.

"Been on the booze, eh?" he said to Chelkash, giving a tug at his trousers.

"You're right, baby-face, you're right," confessed Chelkash with a smile. He was instantly drawn to this wholesome good-natured chap with eyes as clear as a baby's. "Been haymaking?"

"Yes. Made hay, but no money. Times are bad. You never saw so many people! They all come drifting down from the famine districts. No point in working for such pay. Sixty kopeks in the Kuban, think of that! They say they used to pay three or four rubles, or even five."

"Used to! They used to pay three rubles just to get a look at a Russian! That's how I earned a living ten years ago. I'd come to a Cossack village: 'Here I am, folks, an honest-to-God Russian!' They'd all crowd round, look me over, poke me, pinch me, oh-and-ah and pay me three rubles. Give me food and drink besides and invite me to stay as long as I liked."

At first the boy opened wide his mouth, an expression of wondering admiration on his round face, but as he realized Chelkash was fabricating, he snapped his mouth shut, then burst out laughing again. Chelkash kept a straight face, hiding his smile in his moustache.

"A queer bird you are, talking talk as if it was God's truth and me swallowing it. But honest to goodness, it used to be——"

"Isn't that just what I was saying? It used to be——"

"Oh, come!" said the boy with a wave of his hand. "What are you, a cobbler, or a tailor, or what?"

"Me?" Chelkash mused awhile and then said: "I'm a fisherman."

"A fisherman? Think of that! So you catch fish, do you?"

"Why fish? The fishermen here don't only catch fish. Mostly dead bodies, old anchors, sunken boats. There's special fishhooks for such things."

"Lying again. Maybe you're one of those fishermen who sing:

We cast our nets
Upon the shores,
In market stalls, in open doors.

"Ever met fishermen like that?" asked Chelkash, looking hard at the boy and grinning.

"No, but I've heard about them."

"Like the idea?"

"Of people like that? Why not? At least they're free; they can do what they please."

"What's freedom to you? Do you hanker after freedom?"

"Of course. What could be better than to be your own boss, go where you like and do what you like? Only you've got to keep straight and see that no millstones get hung round your neck. Outside of that, go ahead and have a good time without a thought for anything save God and your conscience."

Chelkash spat contemptuously and turned away.

"Here's what I'm up against," went on the boy. "My father died without leaving anything much, my mother's old, the land's sucked dry. What am I supposed to do? I've got to go on living, but how? God knows. I have a chance to marry into a good family. I wouldn't mind if they'd give the daughter her portion. But they won't. Her old man won't give her an inch of land. So I'd have to work for him, and for a long time. For years. There you are. If only I could lay hands on, say, a hundred and fifty rubles I'd be able to stand up to her father and say: 'Do you want me to marry your Marfa? You don't? Just as you say; she's not the only girl in the village, thank God.' I'd be independent, see? and could do what I liked." The boy heaved a sigh. "But it looks as if there was nothing for it but to be his son-in-law. I thought I'd bring back a couple of hundred rubles from the Kuban. That would be the thing! Then I'd be a gentleman! But I didn't earn a damn thing. Nothing for it but to be a farmhand. I'll never have a farm of my own. So there you are."

The boy squirmed and his face fell at the prospect of being this man's son-in-law.

"Where you bound now?" asked Chelkash.

"Home. Where else?"

"How do I know? Maybe you're bound for Turkey."

"Turkey?" marveled the boy. "What honest Christian would ever go to Turkey? A fine thing to say!"

"You *are* a blockhead," murmured Chelkash, turning away again. Yet this wholesome village lad had stirred something in him; a vague feeling of dissatisfaction was slowly taking form within him, and this kept him from concentrating his mind on the night's task.

The boy, offended by Chelkash's words, muttered to himself and threw sidelong glances at the older man. His cheeks were puffed up in a droll way, his lips were pouting and his narrowed eyes blinked rapidly. Evidently he had not expected his talk with this bewhiskered ruffian tramp to end so suddenly and so unsatisfactorily.

But the tramp paid no more attention to him. His mind was on something else as he sat there on the curbstone whistling to himself and beating time with a dirty toe.

The boy wanted to get even with him.

"Hey, you fisherman! Do you often go on a bout?" he began, but at that moment the fisherman turned to him impulsively and said:

"Look, baby-face, would you like to help me to do a job tonight? Make up your mind, quick!"

"What sort of job?" asked the boy dubiously.

" 'What sort'! Whatever sort I give you. We're going fishing. You'll row."

"Oh, I wouldn't mind doing that, I'm not afraid of work. Only—what if you get me into trouble? You're a queer bird; there's no understanding you."

Chelkash had a sensation as of heartburn.

"Don't go spouting on things you don't know anything

about," he said with cold animosity. "I'll give you a good crack over the bean, and then you'll understand a thing or two."

He jumped up, his eyes flashing, his left hand pulling at his moustache, his right clenched in a hard and corded fist.

The boy was frightened. He glanced quickly about him and then he, too, jumped up, blinking nervously. The two of them stood there silently measuring each other with their eyes.

"Well?" said Chelkash harshly. He was seething inside, twitching all over from the insult taken from this puppy he had held in such contempt so far, but whom he now hated with all his soul because he had such clear blue eyes, such a healthy tanned face, such short sturdy arms; because he had a native village and a house there, and an offer to be the son-in-law of a well-to-do muzhik; he hated him for the way he had lived in the past and would live in the future, but most of all he hated him because he, a mere child as compared with Chelkash, dared to hanker after a freedom he could neither appreciate nor have need of. It is always unpleasant to discover that a person you consider beneath you loves or hates the same things you do, thereby establishing a certain resemblance to yourself.

As the lad looked at Chelkash he recognized in him a master.

"I don't really—er—mind," he said. "After all, I'm looking for work. What difference does it make whether I work for you or somebody else? I just said that because—well, you don't look much like a workingman. You're so—er—down at heel. But that can happen to anybody, I know. God, haven't I seen drunks before? Plenty of them, some even worse than you."

"All right, all right. So you're willing?" said Chelkash in a milder tone.

"With pleasure. State your price."

"The price depends on the job. How much we catch. Maybe you'll get five rubles."

Now that the talk was of money, the peasant wanted to be exact and demanded the same exactness from the man who was hiring him. Once more he had his doubts and suspicions.

"That won't suit me, brother."

Chelkash played his part.

"Don't let's talk about it now. Come along to the tavern."

And they walked down the street side by side, Chelkash twirling his moustache with the air of a master; the lad fearful and distrusting, but willing to comply.

"What's your name?" asked Chelkash.

"Gavrilla," answered the lad.

On entering the dingy, smoke-blackened tavern, Chelkash went up to the bar and in the offhand tone of a frequenter ordered a bottle of vodka, cabbage soup, roast beef and tea. He repeated the list and then said nonchalantly: "On tick," to which the barman replied by nodding silently. This instantly inspired Gavrilla with respect for his employer, who, despite his disreputable appearance, was evidently well known and trusted.

"Now we'll have a bite and talk things over. Sit here and wait for me; I'll be right back."

And he went out. Gavrilla looked about him. The tavern was in a basement; it was dark and damp and filled with the stifling smell of vodka, tobacco smoke, pitch, and something else just as pungent. A drunken red-bearded sailor smeared all over with pitch and coal dust was sprawling at a table opposite him. Between hiccups he gurgled a song made of snatches of words which were all sibilant one minute, all guttural the next. Evidently he was not a Russian.

Behind him were two Moldavian women. Swarthy, dark-haired, ragged, they too were wheezing out a drunken song.

Out of shadows loomed other figures, all of them noisy, restless, dishevelled, drunken. . . .

Gavrilla was gripped by fear. If only his boss would come back! The noises of the tavern merged in a single voice, and it was as if some huge multiple-tongued beast were roaring as it vainly sought a means of escape from this stone pit. Gavrilla felt some intoxication seeping into his body, making his head swim and his eyes grow hazy as they roved the tavern with fearful curiosity.

At last Chelkash came back and the two men began to eat and drink and talk. Gavrilla was drunk after his third glass of vodka. He felt very gay and was anxious to say something nice to this prince of a chap who had treated him to such a fine meal. But somehow the words that surged in his throat would not come off his tongue, suddenly grown thick and unwieldy.

Chelkash looked at him with a condescending smile.

"Stewed? Ekh, you rag! On five swigs. How are you going to work tonight?"

"Ol pal!" lisped Gavrilla. "Don't be 'fraid. I'll show you. Gimme a kiss, c'mon."

"That's all right. Here, take another guzzle."

Gavrilla went on drinking until he reached the point at which everything about him seemed to be moving up and down in rhythmic waves. This was unpleasant and made him sick. His face wore an expression of foolish solemnity. Whenever he tried to say anything, his lips slapped together comically and garbled sounds came through them. Chelkash twisted his moustache and smiled glumly as he gazed at him abstractedly, his mind on something else.

Meanwhile the tavern was roaring as drunkenly as ever. The red-headed sailor had folded his arms on the table and fallen fast asleep.

"Time to go," said Chelkash, getting up.

Gavrilla tried to follow him but could not; he let out an oath and laughed idiotically, as drunks do.

"What a washout!" muttered Chelkash, sitting down again.

Gavrilla kept on laughing and looking at his boss with bleary eyes, while Chelkash turned a sharp and thoughtful eye on him. He saw before him a man whose fate he held in his wolfish paw. Chelkash sensed that he could do what he pleased with him. He could crush him in his hand like a playing card, or he could help him get back to the solid peasant way of life. Conscious of his power over him, he reflected that this lad would never have to drink the cup it had been the fate of him, Chelkash, to drink. He envied and pitied the boy; he despised him, and yet he was sorry to think that he might fall into other hands, no better than his own. In the end, Chelkash's various emotions combined to form a single one that was both fatherly and practical. He pitied the boy and he needed him. And so he took Gavrilla under the arms and lifted him up, giving him little pushes with his knee as he led him out into the tavern yard where he laid him down in the shade of a woodpile, he himself sitting beside him and smoking his pipe. Gavrilla tossed about awhile, gave a few grunts and fell asleep.

III

"Ready?" whispered Chelkash to Gavrilla, who was fussing with the oars.

"In a minute. The oarlock's loose. Can I give it a bang with the oar?"

"No! Not a sound! Push it down with your hands; it'll slip into place."

Both of them were noiselessly busy with a boat tied to the stern of one of a whole fleet of barges loaded with oaken staves and of Turkish feluccas carrying palm and sandal wood and thick cypress logs.

The night was dark, heavy banks of tattered clouds floated across the sky, the sea was calm and black and as heavy as oil.

It gave off a moist saline odor and made tender little noises as it lapped at the shore and the sides of ships, causing Chelkash's boat to rock gently. At some distance from shore could be seen the dark outlines of ships against the sky, their masts tipped by varicolored lights. The sea reflected these lights and was strewn with innumerable yellow spots that looked very beautiful quivering upon the background of black velvet. The sea was sleeping as soundly as a workman who has been worn out by the day's labor.

"Let's go," said Gavrilla, dipping an oar into the water.

"Let's." Chelkash pushed off hard with the steering oar, sending the boat into the lanes between the barges. It glided swiftly over the water, which gave off a blue phosphorescent glow wherever the oars struck it and formed a glowing ribbon in the wake of the boat.

"How's your head? Ache?" asked Chelkash solicitously.

"Something fierce. And it's heavy as lead. Here, I'll wet it."

"What for? Wet your insides; that'll bring you round quicker," said Chelkash, holding out a bottle.

"Ah, God be thanked."

There was a gurgling sound.

"Hey! That's enough!" interrupted Chelkash.

Once more the boat darted forward, weaving its way among the other craft swiftly and soundlessly. Suddenly it was beyond them, and the sea—the mighty boundless sea—stretched far away to the dark-blue horizon, from which sprang billowing clouds: gray-and-mauve with fluffy yellow edges; greenish, the color of sea water; leaden-hued, throwing dark and dreary shadows. Slowly moved the clouds across the sky, now overtaking each other, merging in color and form, annihilating each other only to appear again in new aspects grimly magnificent. There was something fatal in the slow movement of these inanimate forms. It seemed as if there were endless numbers

of them at the rim of the sea, and as if they would go on
crawling across the sky forever, impelled by a vicious desire to
keep the sky from gazing down upon the slumbering sea with
its millions of golden orbs, the many-hued stars, that hung
there alive and pensively radiant, inspiring lofty aspirations in
the hearts of men to whom their pure shining was a precious
thing.

"Nice, the sea, isn't it?" asked Chelkash.

"I suppose so, but it makes me afraid," said Gavrilla as he
pulled hard and evenly on the oars. The water let out a faint
ring and splash as the oars struck it, and it still gave off that
blue phosphorescent glow.

"Afraid! You *are* a boob," grunted Chelkash.

He, a thief, loved the sea. His nervous, restive nature, always
thirsting for new impressions, never had enough of contemplating its dark expanses, so free, so powerful, so boundless.
And he resented such a tepid response to his question about
the beauty of the thing he loved. As he sat there in the stern
of the boat letting his steering oar cut through the water while
he gazed calmly ahead, he was filled with the one desire to
travel as long and as far as he could over that velvety surface.

He always had a warm expansive feeling when he was on
the sea. It filled his whole being, purging it of the dross of daily
life. He appreciated this and liked to see himself a better man
here among the waves and in the open air, where thoughts
about life lose their poignancy and life itself loses it value. At
night the soft breathing of the slumbering sea is wafted gently
over the waters, and this boundless sound fills the heart of man
with peace, crams away its evil impulses, and gives birth to
great dreams.

"Where's the fishing tackle?" asked Gavrilla suddenly,
glancing anxiously about the boat.

Chelkash gave a start.

"The tackle? I've got it here in the stern."

He did not wish to lie to this green youth and he regretted having his thoughts and feelings dispelled in this abrupt way. It made him angry. Again he had that burning sensation in his throat and chest and said to Gavrilla in a hard and impressive voice:

"Listen, sit where you are and mind your own business. I hired you to row, so you row; and if you start wagging your tongue it will go hard with you. Understand?"

The boat gave a little jerk and came to a halt, the oars dragging and stirring up the water. Gavrilla shifted uneasily on his seat.

"Row!"

A fierce oath shook the air. Gavrilla lifted the oars and the boat, as if frightened, leaped ahead in quick nervous spurts that made the water splash.

"Steady!"

Chelkash half rose without letting go of the steering oar and fastened cold eyes on Gavrilla's white face. He was like a cat about to spring as he stood there bent forward. The grinding of his teeth could be heard, as could the chattering of Gavrilla's teeth.

"Who's shouting there?" came a stern cry from out at sea.

"Row, you bastard! Row! Shhh! I'll kill you, damn your hide! Row, I tell you! One, two! Just you dare to make a sound! I'll rip you to pieces!" hissed Chelkash.

"Holy Virgin, Mother of God!" murmured Gavrilla, trembling with fear and exertion.

The boat swung round and went back to the harbor where the ships' lanterns formed clusters of colored lights and their masts stood out distinctly.

"Hi! Who's shouting?" came the cry again.

But it came from a distance now. Chelkash was reassured.

"It's you who's shouting!" he called back, then turned to Gavrilla who was still muttering a prayer.

"Luck's with you this time, lad. If those devils had chased us it would have been all over with you. I'd have fed you to the fishes first thing."

Seeing that Chelkash had calmed down and was in a good humor, the trembling Gavrilla pleaded with him:

"Let me go; for the love of Christ, let me go. Set me down somewheres. Oi, oi, oi, I've been trapped! For God's sake, let me go. What do you want of me? I can't do this. I've never been mixed up in such business. It's the first time. God, I'm lost for sure. Why have you done this to me? It's a sin. You'll pay for it with your soul. Oh, what a business!"

"Business?" asked Chelkash sharply. "What business?"

He was amused by the boy's terror; he took pleasure in contemplating it and in thinking what a ferocious fellow he himself was.

"Bad business, brother. Let me go, for the love of God. What do you need me for? Come, be a good chap——"

"Hold your tongue! If I didn't need you I wouldn't have brought you, understand? So shut up!"

"Dear God," murmured Gavrilla.

"Stop blubbering," Chelkash cut him off sharply.

But Gavrilla could no longer control himself; he whimpered softly, coughed, sniffled, wriggled, but rowed with a strength born of despair. The boat flew ahead like an arrow. Once more they found themselves surrounded by the dark forms of ships. Their boat became lost among them as it turned and twisted through the narrow lanes of water.

"Listen, you! If you get asked any questions, keep your mouth shut if you value your life, understand?"

"God!" breathed Gavrilla, adding bitterly: "It must be my fate."

"Stop blubbering," whispered Chelkash again.

This whisper robbed Gavrilla of his mental power; he was benumbed by a chill premonition of disaster. Like one in a trance he dropped his oars into the water, threw himself backwards as he pulled, lifted them and dropped them again, his eyes fixed steadily on his bast sandals.

The sleepy plash of the waves was dreary and terrifying. But now they were in the docks. From the other side of a stone wall came the sound of human voices, of singing and whistling and a splashing of water.

"Stop," whispered Chelkash. "Put down your oars. Push with your hands against the wall. Shhh, damn you!"

Gavrilla guided the boat along the wall by holding on to the slippery masonry. The boat moved without a sound, the slime on the stones deadening the sound of its bumping.

"Stop. Give me the oars; give them to me, I say. Where's your passport? In your knapsack? Let's have it. Hurry up. That's to keep you from running away, pal. No danger of that now. You might have run away without the oars, but not without your passport. Wait here. And mind, if you blab, I'll find you even if it's at the bottom of the sea!"

And then, pulling himself up by his hands, Chelkash disappeared over the wall.

It happened so quickly that Gavrilla gave a little gasp. And then the heaviness in his heart and the fear inspired by that lean bewhiskered thief fell from him like a garment. Now he would run away! Drawing a free breath, he glanced round. To his left rose a black hull without a mast, a sort of gigantic coffin, empty and abandoned. Every time the waves struck it, it let out a hollow sound that might have been a groan. To the left was the slimy wall of the breakwater, a cold heavy serpent uncoiled upon the sea. Behind him loomed other dark forms, while ahead, in the opening between the wall and the coffin, he got a glimpse of the empty sea with black clouds banked above it. Ponderous, enormous, they moved slowly across the sky, spreading horror in the darkness, threatening to crush human beings with their great weight. Everything was cold, black, sinister. Gavrilla was frightened. And his present fear was greater than that inspired by Chelkash. It clamped him tightly round the chest, squeezing all resistance out of him and pinning him to his seat.

Everything was quiet. Not a sound was to be heard but the sighing of the sea. The clouds moved as slowly and drearily as ever, and so many of them rose out of the sea that the sky was like a sea itself, an agitated sea turned upside down over this smooth, slumbering one. The clouds were like waves whose foamy crests were rushing down upon the earth, rushing back into the chasms out of which they had sprung, rushing upon the newborn billows which had not yet broken into the greenish foam of savage fury.

So oppressed was Gavrilla by the austere silence and beauty about him that he was anxious to have his master come back. What if he should not come? Time dragged slowly—slower than the movement of the clouds across the sky. And the longer he waited, the more menacing grew the silence. But at last a splash, a rustle, and something like a whisper came from the other side of the breakwater. Gavrilla felt that he would die in another minute.

"Hullo! Sleeping? Here, catch this. Careful," came the muffled voice of Chelkash.

Something square and heavy was let down over the wall. Gavrilla put it in the boat. A similar bundle followed. Then the lanky form of Chelkash slid down, the oars appeared, Gavrilla's knapsack fell at his feet, and Chelkash, breathing hard, took his seat in the stern.

Gavrilla gave a diffident smile of joy.

"Tired?" he asked.

"Ra-ther! Well, lay on the oars. Pull with all your might. You've earned a neat little sum. Half the job's over; all you've got to do now is slip past those bastards and then—collect and go back to your Masha. I s'pose you've got a Masha, haven't you?"

"N-no." Gavrilla was putting forth his best effort, his lungs working like bellows, his arms like steel springs. The water gurgled under the boat and the blue ribbon in its wake was wider than before. Gavrilla became drenched in sweat but he did not let up on the oars. Twice that night he had a great fright; he did not wish to have a third one. The only thing he wanted was to get this accursed job over as quickly as possible, set foot on dry land and escape from that man while he was still alive and out of jail. He resolved not to talk to him, not to oppose him in any way, to do everything he ordered him to, and if he managed to get away safely, to say a prayer to St. Nicholas the Miracle-Worker on the very next day. An impassioned prayer was ready on his tongue, but he held it back, panting like a locomotive and glancing up at Chelkash from under drawn brows.

Chelkash, long and lean, was crouching like a bird about to take wing, his hawk-like eyes piercing the darkness ahead, his hooked nose sniffing the air, one hand clutching the steering oar, the other pulling at his moustache, which twitched as his thin lips spread in a smile. Chelkash was pleased with his haul, with himself, and with this youth whom he had terrorized and converted into his slave. As he watched Gavrilla exerting himself, he felt sorry for him and thought he would offer him a word of encouragement.

"Ekh!" he said softly, with a little laugh, "got a good scare, did you?"

"Not so bad," grunted Gavrilla.

"You can take it easier now. The danger's over. There's just one place more we've got to slip past. Take a rest."

Gavrilla obediently stopped rowing, and dropped his oars into the water again.

"Row softly. Keep the water from talking. There's a gate we've got to get past. Shhh. The men here can't take a joke. Always ready with their guns. You'll have a hole in your head before you know what's struck you."

Now the boat was gliding through the water almost without sound. The only sign of its movement was the blue shine of the water dripping off the oars and the blue flare of the sea as the drops struck it. The night grew darker and stiller. The sky no longer resembled an agitated sea—the clouds had spread out to form a heavy blanket that hung low and immobile over the water. The sea was even more calm and black, its warm saline odor was stronger than ever, and it no longer seemed so boundless.

"If only it would rain!" murmured Chelkash. "It would hide us like a curtain."

Great forms rose out of the water to right and left of the boat. They were barges—dark and dreary and motionless. On one of them a light could be seen moving: someone was walking about with a lantern in his hand. The sea made little pleading sounds as it patted the sides of the barges, and they gave chill and hollow answers, as if unwilling to grant the favors asked of them.

"A cordon!" said Chelkash in a scarcely audible voice.

Ever since he had told Gavrilla to row softly, the latter had again been gripped by a feeling of tense expectation. As he strained ahead into the darkness it seemed to him that he was growing—his bones and sinews ached as they stretched and his head ached, too, filled as it was with a single thought. The skin of his back quivered and he had a sensation of pins-and-needles in his feet. His eyes felt as if they would burst from straining so hard into the darkness, out of which he expected someone to rise up any minute and shout at them: "Stop, thieves!"

Gavrilla shuddered on hearing Chelkash say "A cordon." A dreadful thought flashed through his mind and struck upon his taut nerves: he thought of calling out for help. He even opened his mouth, pressed his chest against the side of the boat and took a deep breath, but horror of what he was about to do struck him like a lash; he closed his eyes and fell off the seat.

From out of the black waters rose a flaming blue sword of light; rose and cleaved the darkness of night; cut through the clouds in the sky and came to rest on the bosom of the sea in a broad blue ribbon of light. There it lay, its rays picking the forms of ships, hitherto unseen, out of the darkness—black silent forms, shrouded in the gloom of night. It was as if these ships had lain for long at the bottom of the sea, to which they had been consigned by the forces of the storm, and now, at the will of this flaming sword born of the sea, they had been raised, that they might gaze on the sky and on all things that exist above water. The rigging of their masts was like clinging sea-weed that had been brought up from the bottom of the sea along with the gigantic black forms it enmeshed as in a net. Then once again this fearsome blue sword rose, flashing, off the bosom of the sea, and once again it cleaved the night and lay down again, this time in another spot. And again the forms of ships which had not been seen before were illuminated by its light.

Chelkash's boat stopped and rocked on the water as if deliberating what to do. Gavrilla was lying in the bottom of the boat, his hands over his face, while Chelkash poked him with his foot and whispered savagely:

"That's the customs cruiser, you fool! And that's its spotlight. Get up. They'll have it pointed at us in a minute. You'll be the ruin of me and yourself as well, you idiot. Get up!"

A particularly effective kick in the back brought Gavrilla to his feet. Still afraid to open his eyes, he sat down, felt for the oars, and began to row.

"Easy! Easy, damn you! God, what a fool I picked up! What you afraid of, snout-face? A lantern—that's all it is. Easy with those oars, God damn you! They're searching for smugglers. But they won't catch us. They're too far out. Oh, no, they won't catch us. Now we're—" Chelkash looked about triumphantly "—we're out of danger. Phew! Well, you're a lucky devil, even if you are a blockhead."

Gavrilla rowed on, saying nothing, breathing heavily, stealing sidelong glances at the flaming sword that kept rising and falling. Chelkash said it was only a lantern, but he could not believe it. There was something uncanny about this cold blue light cleaving the darkness, giving the sea a silver shimmer, and once more Gavrilla was gripped by fear. He rowed mechanically, all his muscles taut as in expectation of a blow from above, and there was nothing he wanted now; he was empty and inanimate. The excitement of that night had drained everything human out of him.

But Chelkash was jubilant. His nerves, used to strain, quickly relaxed. His moustache twitched with gratification and his eyes sparkled. Never had he been in better humor; he whistled through his teeth, drew in deep breaths of the moist sea air, looked about him, smiled good-naturedly when his eyes came to rest on Gavrilla.

A wind sprang up, rousing the sea and covering it with little ripples. The clouds grew thinner and more transparent but the whole sky was still covered with them. The wind rushed lightly back and forth across the sea, but the clouds hung motionless, as if deeply engrossed in drab, uninteresting thoughts.

"Come, snap out of it, brother. You look as if you'd had all the spirit knocked out of you; nothing but a bag of bones left. As if it was the end of the world."

Gavrilla was glad to hear a human voice, even if it was Chelkash's.

"I'm all right," he murmured.

"You look it! Got no stuffings in you. Here, take the steering oar and let me row. You must be tired."

Gavrilla got up mechanically and changed places with him. In passing, Chelkash got a look at the boy's white face and noticed that his knees were trembling so that they could hardly hold him. This made him more sorry than ever for him, and he gave him a pat on the shoulder.

"Come, chin up! You did a good job. I'll reward you well for it. What would you think if I handed you a twenty-five ruble note, eh?"

"I don't want anything. Nothing but to get on shore."

Chelkash gave a wave of his hand, spat, and began to row, swinging the oars far back with his long arms.

The sea was quite awake now. It amused itself by making little waves, ornamenting them with fringes of foam, and running them into each other so that they broke in showers of spray. The foam hissed and sighed as it dissolved, and the air was filled with musical sounds. The darkness seemed to have waked up, too.

"So now," said Chelkash, "you'll go back to your village, get married, start working the land, raise corn, your wife will bear children, there won't be enough to eat, and all your life you'll work yourself to the bone. What fun is there in that?"

"Fun?" echoed Gavrilla faintly and with a little shudder.

Here and there the wind tore rifts in the clouds, revealing patches of blue sky set with one or two stars. The reflection of these stars danced on the water, now disappearing, now gleaming again.

"Bear more to the right," said Chelkash. "We're almost there. Hm, the job's over. A big job. Just think, five hundred rubles in a single night!"

"Five hundred?" repeated Gavrilla incredulously. Frightened by the words, he gave the bundles a little kick and said, "What's in them?"

"Things that are worth a lot of money. They'd bring in a thousand if I got the right price, but I can't be bothered. Slick, eh?"

"Good Lord!" said Gavrilla unbelievingly. "If only I had as much!" He sighed as he thought of his village, his wretched farm, his mother, and all those dear and distant things for whose sake he had set out in search of work; for whose sake he had undergone the tortures of that night. He was caught up in a wave of memories—his little village on the side of a hill running down to the river, and the woods above the river with its birches, willows, rowans, and bird-cherry.

"How I need it!" he sighed mournfully.

"You don't say. I s'pose you'd jump straight on a train and make a dash for home. And wouldn't the girls be mad on you! Why, you could have any one of them you liked. And you'd build yourself a new house although the money's hardly enough for a house."

"No, not a house. Timber's dear up our way."

"At least you'd repair the old one. And what about a horse? Have you got a horse?"

"Yes, but it's a feeble old thing."

"So you'll need to buy a new horse. A first-rate horse. And a cow. . . . And some sheep. And some poultry, eh?"

"Ekh, don't mention it! Couldn't I set myself up fine!"

"You could, brother. And life would be like a song. I know a thing or two about such things myself. I had a nest of my own once. My father was one of the richest men in the village."

Chelkash was scarcely rowing. The boat was tossed by the waves splashing mischievously against its sides, and it made almost no progress through the dark waters, now growing more and more playful. The two men sat there rocking and looking about them, each absorbed in his own dreams. Chelkash had reminded Gavrilla of his village in the hope of quieting the boy's nerves and cheering him up. He had done so with his tongue in his cheek, but as he taunted his companion with reminders of the joys of peasant life, joys which he himself had long since ceased to value and had quite forgotten until this moment, he gradually let himself be carried away, and before he knew it he himself was expounding on the subject instead of questioning the boy about the village and its affairs.

"The best thing about peasant life is that a man's free, he's his own boss. He's got his own house, even if it's a poor one. And he's got his own land—maybe only a little patch, but it's his. He's a king, once he's got his own land. He's a man to be reckoned with. He can demand respect from anybody, can't he?" he ended up with animation.

Gavrilla looked at him curiously, and he, too, became animated. In the course of their talk he had forgotten who this man was; he saw in him only another peasant like himself, glued fast to the land by the sweat of many generations of forefathers, bound to it by memories of childhood; a peasant who of his own free choice had severed connections with the land and with labor on the land, for which he had been duly punished.

"True, brother. How very true! Look at you now; what are you without any land? The land, brother, is like your mother; there's no forgetting it."

Chelkash came back to his surroundings. Again he felt that burning sensation in his chest that always troubled him when his pride—the pride of a reckless daredevil—was injured, especially if injured by someone he considered a nonentity.

"Trying to teach me!" he said fiercely. "Did you think I meant what I said? Know your place, upstart!"

"You're a funny one," said Gavrilla with his former timidity. "I didn't mean you. There's lots of others like you. God, how many miserable people there are in the world! Homeless tramps."

"Here, take over the oars," snapped Chelkash, holding back the flood of oaths that surged in his throat.

Once more they exchanged places, and as Chelkash climbed over the bundles he had an irresistible desire to give Gavrilla a push that would send him flying into the water.

They did no more talking, but Gavrilla emanated the breath of the village even when he was silent. Chelkash became so engrossed in thoughts of the past that he forgot to steer, and the current turned the boat out to sea. The waves seemed to sense that this boat was without a pilot, and they played with it gleefully, tossing it on their crests and leaping in little blue flames about the oars. In front of Chelkash's eyes passed a kaleidoscope of the past, of the distant past, separated from the present by the gulf of eleven years of vagrancy. He saw himself as a child, saw his native village, saw his mother, a stout red-cheeked woman with kindly gray eyes, and his father, a stern-faced, red-bearded giant. He saw himself as a bridegroom, and he saw his bride, the plump black-eyed Anfisa with a mild, cheerful disposition and a long plait hanging down her back. Again he saw himself, this time as a handsome Guardsman; again his father, now gray-haired and stooped with labor; and his mother, wrinkled and bent to earth. He saw the reception the village gave him when his army service was over, and he recalled how proud his father had been to show off this healthy, handsome, bewhiskered soldier-son to the neighbors. Memory is the bane of those who have come to misfortune; it brings to life the very stones of the past, and adds a drop of honey even to the bitterest potion drunk at some far time.

It was as if a gentle stream of native air were wafted over Chelkash, bringing to his ears his mother's tender words, his father's earnest peasant speech and many other forgotten sounds; bringing to his nostrils the fragrance of mother-earth as it thawed, as it was new-plowed, as it drew on an emerald coverlet of springing rye. He felt lonely, uprooted, thrown once and for all beyond the pale of that way of life which had produced the blood flowing in his veins.

"Hey, where are we going?" cried Gavrilla.

Chelkash started and glanced about with the alertness of a bird of prey.

"Look where we've drifted, damn it all. Row harder."

"Daydreaming?" smiled Gavrilla.

"Tired."

"No danger of getting caught with them things?" asked Gavrilla, giving the bundles a little kick.

"No, have no fear. I'll turn them in now and get my money."

"Five hundred?"

"At least."

"God, what a pile! If only I had it! Wouldn't I play a pretty tune with it, just!"

"A peasant tune?"

"What else? I'd. . . ."

And Gavrilla soared on the wings of his imagination. Chelkash said nothing. His moustache drooped, his right side had been drenched by a wave, his eyes were sunken and lusterless. All the hawkishness had gone out of him, had been wrung out of him by a humiliating introspection that even glanced out of the folds of his filthy shirt.

He turned the boat sharply about and steered it towards a black form rising out of the water.

Once more the sky was veiled in clouds and a fine warm rain set in, making cheerful little plopping sounds as its drops struck the water.

"Stop! Hold it!" ordered Chelkash.

The nose of the boat ran into the side of a barge.

"Are they asleep or what, the bastards?" growled Chelkash as he slipped a boat hook into some ropes hanging over the side. "Throw down the ladder! And the rain had to wait till this minute to come down! Hey, you sponges! Hey!"

"Selkash?" purred someone on deck.

"Where's the ladder?"

"Kalimera,* Selkash."

"The ladder, God damn you!"

"Oo, what a temper he's in tonight! Eloy!"

"Climb up, Gavrilla," said Chelkash to his companion.

The next minute they were on deck, where three bearded, dark-skinned fellows were talking animatedly in a lisping tongue as they stared over the gunwale into Chelkash's boat. A fourth, wrapped in a long chlamys,† went over to Chelkash and shook his hand without a word, then threw Gavrilla a questioning look.

"Have the money ready in the morning," Chelkash said to him briefly. "I'm going to take a snooze now. Come along, Gavrilla. Are you hungry?"

"I'm sleepy," said Gavrilla. Five minutes later he was snoring loudly while Chelkash sat beside him trying on somebody else's boots, spitting off to one side and whistling a sad tune through his teeth. Presently he stretched out beside Gavrilla with his hands behind his head and lay there with his moustache twitching.

The barge rolled on the waves, a board creaked plaintively, the rain beat on the deck and the waves against the sides of the

* *Kalimera.* (Greek) Good day.
† *chlamys.* A sleeveless coat.

barge. It was all very mournful and reminded one of the cradle song of a mother who has little hope of seeing her child happy.

Chelkash bared his teeth, raised his head, glanced about him, muttered something to himself and lay down again with his legs spread wide apart, making him look like a pair of giant scissors.

IV

He was the first to wake up. He glanced anxiously about him, was instantly reassured, and looked down at Gavrilla, who was snoring happily, a smile spread all over his wholesome, sunburnt, boyish face. Chelkash gave a sigh and climbed up a narrow rope ladder. A patch of lead-colored sky peered down the hatchway. It was light, but the day was dull and dreary, as is often so in autumn.

Chelkash came back in a couple of hours. His face was red and his whiskers had been given a rakish twist. He was wearing a sturdy pair of high boots, a leather hunting jacket and breeches as a hunter wears. The outfit was not new, but in good condition and very becoming to him, since it filled out his figure, rounded off the edges and gave him a certain military air.

"Get up, puppy," said he, giving Gavrilla a little kick.

Gavrilla jumped up only half-awake and gazed at Chelkash with frightened eyes, not recognizing him. Chelkash burst out laughing.

"Don't you look grand!" said Gavrilla with a broad grin at last. "Quite the gentleman."

"That don't take us long. But you're a lily-livered fellow if there ever was one. How many times were you about to pass out last night?"

"You can't blame me; I'd never been on a job like that before. I might have lost my soul."

"Would you do it again, eh?"

"Again? Only if—how shall I put it? What would I get for it?"

"If you got, let's say, two smackers?"

"You mean two hundred rubles? Not bad. I might."

"And what about losing your soul?"

"Maybe I wouldn't lose it after all," grinned Gavrilla.

"You wouldn't lose it, and you'd be fixed up for the rest of your life."

Chelkash laughed gaily.

"Well, enough of joking; let's go ashore."

And so they found themselves in the boat again, Chelkash steering, Gavrilla rowing. Above them stretched a solid canopy of gray clouds; the sea was a dull green and it played joyfully with the boat, tossing it up on waves that had not yet grown to any size, and throwing handfuls of pale spray against its sides. Far up ahead could be glimpsed a strip of yellow sand, while behind them stretched the sea, chopped up into coveys of whitecaps. Behind them, too, were the ships—a whole forest of masts back there to the left, with the white buildings of the port as a background. A dull rumble came pouring out of the port over the sea, mingling with the roar of the waves to form fine strong music. And over everything hung a thin veil of fog that made all objects seem remote.

"Ekh, it'll be something to see by nightfall!" exclaimed Chelkash, nodding out to sea.

"A storm?" asked Gavrilla as he plowed powerfully through the waves with his oars. His clothes were soaked with wind-blown spray.

"Uh-huh," said Chelkash.

Gavrilla looked at him inquisitively.

"Well, how much did they give you?" he asked at last, seeing that Chelkash had no intention of broaching the subject.

"Look," and Chelkash pulled something out of his pocket and held it out.

Gavrilla's eyes were dazzled by the sight of so many crisp bright bank notes.

"And here I was thinking you had lied to me! How much is it?"

"Five hundred and forty."

"Phe-e-w!" gasped Gavrilla, following the course of the notes back to the pocket with greedy eyes. "God! If only I had that much money!" and he gave a doleful sigh.

"You and me'll go on a big spree, mate," cried Chelkash ecstatically. "We'll paint the town red. You'll get your share, never fear. I'll give you forty. That enough, eh? Give it straight away if you want me to."

"All right, I'll take it if you don't mind."

Gavrilla was shaking with anticipation.

"Ekh, you scarecrow, you! 'I'll take it!' Here, go ahead and take it. Take it, damn it all. I don't know what to do with so much money. Do me a favor and take some of it off my hands."

Chelkash held out several notes to Gavrilla, who let go of the oars to clutch them in trembling fingers and thrust them inside his shirt, screwing up his eyes as he did so and taking in great gulps of air as if he had just scalded his throat. Chelkash watched him, a squeamish smile on his lips. Once more Gavrilla picked up the oars and began to row nervously, hurriedly, with his eyes cast down, like a man who has just had a bad fright. His shoulders and ears were twitching.

"You're a greedy bloke. That's no good. But what's to be expected?—you're a peasant," mused Chelkash.

"A man can do anything with money!" exclaimed Gavrilla in a sudden flare of excitement. And then hurriedly, incoherently, chasing his thoughts and catching his words on the fly, he drew the contrast between life in the village with money and without it. Honor, comfort, pleasure!

Chelkash followed him attentively, his face grave, his eyes

narrowed thoughtfully. From time to time he would give a pleased smile.

"Here we are!" he interruped Gavrilla's tirade.

The boat was caught on a wave that drove it into the sand.

"Well, this is the end. But we've got to pull the boat up good and high so that it don't get washed away. Some people will come for it. And now it's good-bye. We're about ten versts from town. You going back to town?"

Chelkash's face was beaming with a sly and good-natured smile, as if he were contemplating something very pleasant for himself and very unexpected for Gavrilla. He thrust his hand into his pocket and rustled the notes there.

"No—I'm not going. I'm—I'm—" Gavrilla stammered as if choking.

Chelkash looked at him.

"What's eating you?" he said.

"Nothing." But Gavrilla's face turned first red, then gray, and he kept shifting on his feet as if he wanted to throw himself at Chelkash or do something else of insuperable difficulty.

Chelkash was nonplussed by the boy's agitation. He waited to see what would come of it.

Gavrilla broke into laughter that sounded more like sobbing. His head was hanging, so that Chelkash could not see the expression of his face, but he could see his ears going from red to white.

"To hell with you," said Chelkash with a disgusted wave of his hand. "Are you in love with me, or what? Squirming like a girl. Or maybe you can't bear to part with me? Speak up, spineless, or I'll just walk off."

"You'll walk off?" shrieked Gavrilla.

The deserted beach trembled at the shriek, and the ripples of yellow sand made up by the washing of the waves seemed to heave. Chelkash himself started. All of a sudden Gavrilla rushed towards Chelkash, threw himself at his feet, seized him round the knees and gave him a tug. Chelkash staggered and sat down heavily in the sand; clenching his teeth, he swung up his long arm with the hand closed in a tight fist. But the blow was intercepted by Gavrilla's pleadings, uttered in a cringing whisper:

"Give me that money, there's a good fellow! For the love of Christ give it to me. What do you need with it? Look, in just one night—in one single night! And it would take me years and years. Give it to me. I'll pray for you. All my life. In three churches. For the salvation of your soul. You'll only throw it to the winds, while I? I'll put it in the land. Give it to me! What is it to you? It comes so easy. One night, and you're a rich man. Do a good deed once in your life. After all, you're a lost soul; there's nothing ahead of you. And I'd—oh what wouldn't I do with it! Give it to me!"

Chelkash—frightened, dumbfounded, infuriated—sat in the sand leaning back on his elbows; sat without a word, his eyes boring into this boy whose head was pressed against his knees as he gasped out his plea. At last Chelkash jumped to his feet, thrust his hand into his pocket and threw the notes at Gavrilla.

"Here, lick it up!" he cried, trembling with excitement, with pity and loathing for this greedy slave. He felt heroic when he had tossed him the money.

"I was going to give you more anyway. Went soft last night thinking of my own village. Thought to myself: I'll help the lad. But I waited to see if you'd ask for it. And you did, you milksop, you beggar, you. Is it worth tormenting yourself like that for money? Fool. Greedy devils. No pride. They'd sell themselves for five kopeks."

"May Christ watch over you! What's this I've got? Why, I'm a rich man now!" squealed Gavrilla, twitching all over in ecstasy and hiding the money inside his shirt. "Bless you, my friend. I'll never forget you. Never. And I'll have my wife and children say prayers for you, too."

As Chelkash heard his joyful squeals and looked at his beaming face distorted by his paroxysm of greed, he realized that, thief and drunk that he was, he would never stoop so low, would never be so grasping, so lacking in self-pride. Never, never! And this thought and this feeling, filling him with a sense of his own freedom, made him linger there beside Gavrilla on the shore of the sea.

"You've made me a present of happiness," cried Gavrilla, snatching Chelkash's hand and pressing it against his own face.

Chelkash bared his teeth like a wolf but said nothing.

"And just to think what I almost did!" went on Gavrilla. "On the way here I thought—to myself—I'll hit him—you, that is—over the head—with an oar—bang!—take the money—and throw him—you, that is—overboard. Who'd ever miss him? And if they found his body—nobody'd bother to find out who did it and how. He's not worth making a fuss over. Nobody needs him. Nobody'd go to the trouble."

"Hand over that money!" roared Chelkash, seizing Gavrilla by the throat.

Gavrilla wrenched away once, twice, but Chelkash's arm wound about him like a snake. The sound of a shirt ripping, and—there was Gavrilla flat on his back in the sand, his eyes popping out of his head, his fingers clutching the air, his feet kicking helplessly. Chelkash stood over him, lean, erect, hawklike, his teeth bared as he gave a hard dry laugh, his whiskers twitching nervously on his sharp bony face. Never in all his life had he been wounded so cruelly, and never had he been so furious.

"Well, are you happy now?" he laughed, then turned on his heel and set off in the direction of the town. Before he had gone five steps Gavrilla arched himself like a cat, sprang to his feet, swung out with his arm and hurled a big stone at him.

"Take that!"

Chelkash let out a grunt, put his hands to his head, staggered forward, turned round to Gavrilla, and fell on his face in the sand. Gavrilla was frozen with fear. Chelkash moved one leg, tried to lift his head, stretched out, trembling like a harp string. Then Gavrilla ran for all he was worth, ran out into the dark space where a shaggy black cloud was hanging over the fog-enshrouded steppe. The waves rustled as they scurried up the sand, mingled with the sand for a brief moment, scurried back again. The foam hissed and the air was filled with spray.

It began to rain. At first it came down in single drops, but soon turned into a torrent that came pouring out of the sky in thin streams. These streams wove a net of watery threads that enveloped the whole expanse of the steppe, the whole expanse of the sea. Gavrilla was swallowed up in it. For a long time nothing was to be seen but the rain and the long figure of the man lying in the sand at the edge of the sea. Then Gavrilla came swooping like a bird out of the darkness. When he reached Chelkash he fell on his knees beside him and tried to lift him up. His hand came in contact with something warm and red and sticky. He shuddered and started back, with a wild expression on his white face.

"Get up, brother, get up!" he whispered in Chelkash's ear above the noise of the rain.

Chelkash opened his eyes and gave Gavrilla a little push.

"Go away," he whispered hoarsely.

"Brother! Forgive me! It was the devil's doings," whispered Gavrilla trembling as he kissed Chelkash's hand.

"Go away. Leave me."

"Take this sin off my soul. Forgive me, brother."

"Away! Go away! Go to hell!" Chelkash suddenly cried out

and sat up in the sand. His face was white and angry, his eyes were hazy and kept closing as if he were sleepy. "What else do you want? You've done what you wanted to do. Go away. Get out!" He tried to give the grief-stricken Gavrilla a kick, but he could not and would have collapsed again had not Gavrilla put an arm round his shoulders. Chelkash's face was on a level with Gavrilla's. Both faces were white and dreadful to see.

"Bah!" And Chelkash spat into the wide-open eyes of his assistant.

Gavrilla humbly wiped his face on his sleeve.

"Do what you want to me," he whispered. "I won't say a word. Forgive me, in the name of Christ."

"Scum. Can't even do your dirty work like a man," cried Chelkash scathingly as he slipped his hand inside his jacket and ripped off a piece of shirt with which he silently bound his head, grinding his teeth from time to time. "Have you taken the money?" he asked through his teeth.

"I haven't, brother. And I won't. I don't want it. Nothing but bad luck comes of it."

Chelkash thrust his hand into a pocket of his jacket, pulled out the pile of notes, peeled off a hundred-ruble one, put it back into his pocket, and threw the rest at Gavrilla.

"Take it and go away."

"I won't, brother. I can't. Forgive me what I've done."

"Take it, I say," roared Chelkash, rolling his eyes fearfully.

"Forgive me. I can't take it if you don't," said Gavrilla humbly, falling at Chelkash's feet in the rain-drenched sand.

"That's a lie. You will take it, you scum," said Chelkash with conviction. Pulling up his companion's head by the hair, he thrust the money under his nose.

"Take it. Take it. You didn't work for nothing. Don't be afraid, take it. And don't be ashamed that you almost killed a man. Nobody would hunt you down for killing a man like me. They'd even say thank you if they found out. Here, take it."

Seeing that Chelkash was laughing, Gavrilla's heart grew lighter. He clutched the money.

"And do you forgive me, brother? Don't you want to do that for me?" he begged tearfully.

"My beloved friend," replied Chelkash in the same vein, as he got up and stood swaying on his feet. "What's there to forgive? Nothing to forgive. Today you get me; tomorrow I get you."

"Ah brother, brother," sighed Gavrilla disconsolately, shaking his head.

Chelkash stood in front of him with an odd smile on his face. The rag on his head, which had gradually been getting redder, resembled a Turkish fez.

The rain had become a downpour. The sea gave a low roar, the waves hurled themselves savagely at the shore.

The two men were silent.

"Well, good-bye," said Chelkash mockingly as he turned to go.

He staggered, his legs were shaking, and he held his head as if afraid of losing it.

"Forgive me, brother," pleaded Gavrilla once more.

"That's all right," said Chelkash coldly, setting off.

He stumbled away, holding his head with his left hand, pulling gently at his dark moustache with his right.

Gavrilla stood watching him until he disappeared in the rain which kept coming down in fine endless streams, enveloping the steppe in impenetrable steel-gray gloom.

Then he took off his wet cap, crossed himself, looked at the money in his hand, heaved a deep sigh of relief, hid the money in his shirt, and strode off firmly down the shore in the opposite direction to that taken by Chelkash.

The sea growled as it hurled its huge waves on the sand, smashing them to foam and spray. The rain lashed at the water and the land. The wind howled. The air was filled with a roar, a howl, a murmur. The rain cut off sight of sea and sky.

Soon the rain and the spray washed away the red spot on the sand where Chelkash had lain, washed away the footsteps of Chelkash, washed away the footsteps of the youth who had walked so bravely down the beach. And not a sign was left on this deserted shore to testify to the little drama enacted here by these two men.

Interpretive Questions

1. Why does Gorky begin his story by showing the dock worker "slaves" and the turmoil of the harbor?

2. Why does the author have Chelkash choose a means of livelihood that normally requires "little effort" but "a great deal of skill"?

3. Why does the author choose Chelkash—a thief, a drunkard, and a "character"—to represent freedom?

4. Why does Gavrilla come back to Chelkash after knocking him out?

5. Does Chelkash forgive Gavrilla?

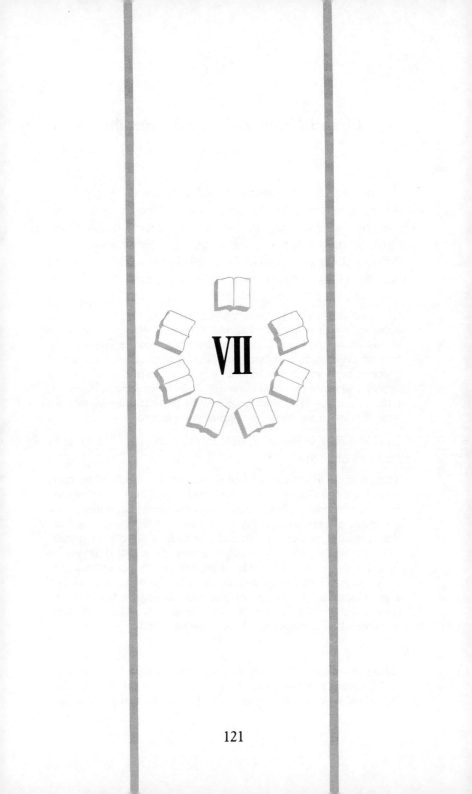

VII

By and About Alexis de Tocqueville

(1805–1859)

From May 1831 to February 1832, Alexis de Tocqueville observed democratic politics and society as he traveled in the United States. *Democracy in America,* the record of his observations, brought Tocqueville international recognition.

After a month of travel, Tocqueville wrote to his father about the relative value of political institutions:

> The more I see this country the more I admit myself penetrated with this truth: that there is nothing absolute in the theoretical value of political institutions, and that their efficiency depends almost always on the original circumstances and the social condition of the people to whom they are applied. I see institutions succeed here which would infallibly turn France upside down; others which suit us would obviously do harm in America; and yet, either I am much mistaken, or man is neither other nor better here than with us. Only he is otherwise placed.

In *Democracy in America,* he commented on self-interest in relation to morality:

> The principle of self-interest rightly understood produces no great acts of self-sacrifice, but it suggests daily small acts of self-denial. By itself it cannot suffice to make a man virtuous; but it disciplines a number of persons in habits of regularity, temperance, moderation, foresight, self-command; and if it does not lead men straight to virtue by the will, it gradually draws them in that direction by their habits.... The principle of interest rightly understood perhaps prevents men from rising far above the level of mankind, but a great number of other men, who were falling far below it, are caught and restrained by it. Observe some few individuals, they are lowered by it; survey mankind, they are raised.

On majority rule:

> A majority taken collectively is only an individual whose opinions, and frequently whose interests, are opposed to those of another individual who is styled a minority. If it be admitted that a man

possessing absolute power may misuse that power by wronging his adversaries, why should not a majority be liable to the same reproach?

On reelecting the president:

It is impossible to consider the ordinary course of affairs in the United States without perceiving that the desire to be re-elected is the chief aim of the President; that the whole policy of his administration, and even his most indifferent measures, tend to this object; and that, especially as the crisis approaches, his personal interest takes the place of his interest in the public good. The principle of re-eligibility renders the corrupting influence of elective government still more extensive and pernicious.

In the selection that follows, Tocqueville considers the paradox that democracy, which calls for the destruction of class distinctions, opens the door for a system in which classes of people are economically interdependent but not bound to one another by loyalty, custom, or duty.

How an Aristocracy May Be Created by Industry

Alexis de Tocqueville

I have shown how democracy favors the development of industry by multiplying without limit the number of those engaged therein. We shall now see by what roundabout route industry may in turn lead men back to aristocracy.

It is acknowledged that when a workman spends every day on the same detail, the finished article is produced more easily, quickly, and economically.

It is likewise acknowledged that the larger the scale on which an industrial undertaking is conducted with great capital assets and extensive credit, the cheaper will its products be.

People had formed some inkling of these truths long ago, but it is in our day that they have been demonstrated. They have already been applied to several very important industries, and in due turn even the smallest will take advantage of them.

---

*A selection from *Democracy in America*.

There is nothing in the world of politics that deserves the lawgivers' attention more than these two new axioms of industrial science.

When a workman is constantly and exclusively engaged in making one object, he ends by performing this work with singular dexterity. But at the same time, he loses the general faculty of applying his mind to the way he is working. Every day he becomes more adroit and less industrious, and one may say that in his case the man is degraded as the workman improves.

What is one to expect from a man who has spent twenty years of his life making heads for pins? And how can he employ that mighty human intelligence which has so often stirred the world, except in finding out the best way of making heads for pins?

When a workman has spent a considerable portion of his life in this fashion, his thought is permanently fixed on the object of his daily toil; his body has contracted certain fixed habits which it can never shake off. In a word, he no longer belongs to himself, but to his chosen calling. In vain are all the efforts of law and morality to break down the barriers surrounding such a man and open up a thousand different roads to fortune for him on every side. An industrial theory stronger than morality or law ties him to a trade, and often to a place, which he cannot leave. He has been assigned a certain position in society which he cannot quit. In the midst of universal movement, he is struck immobile.

As the principle of the division of labor is ever more completely applied, the workman becomes weaker, more limited, and more dependent. The craft improves, the craftsman slips back. On the other hand, as it becomes ever clearer that the products of industry become better and cheaper as factories become vaster and capital greater, very rich and well-educated men come forward to exploit industries which, up to that time, had been left to ignorant and rough artisans. They are attracted by the scale of the efforts required and the importance of the results to be achieved.

Thus, at the same time that industrial science constantly lowers the standing of the working class, it raises that of the masters.

While the workman confines his intelligence more and more to studying one single detail, the master daily embraces a vast field in his vision, and his mind expands as fast as the other's contracts. Soon the latter will need no more than bodily strength without intelligence, while to succeed the former needs science and almost genius. The former becomes more and more like the administrator of a huge empire, and the latter more like a brute.

So there is no resemblance between master and workman, and daily they become more different. There is no connection except that between the first and last links in a long chain. Each occupies a place made for him, from which he does not move. One is in a state of constant, narrow, and necessary dependence on the other and seems to have been born to obey, as the other was to command.

What is this, if not an aristocracy?

As conditions become more and more equal in the body of the nation, the need for manufactured products becomes greater and more general, and the cheapness which brings these things within reach of men of moderate fortune becomes an ever greater element in success.

Thus there is a constant tendency for very rich and well-educated men to devote their wealth and knowledge to manufactures and to seek, by opening large establishments with a strict division of labor, to meet the fresh demands which are made on all sides.

Hence, just while the mass of the nation is turning toward democracy, that particular class which is engaged in industry becomes more aristocratic. Men appear more and more like in the one context and more and more different in the other, and inequality increases within the little society in proportion as it decreases in society at large.

It would thus appear, tracing things back to their source, that a natural impulse is throwing up an aristocracy out of the bosom of democracy.

But that aristocracy is not at all like those that have preceded it.

First, be it noted that because it only flourishes in industry and in some industrial callings, it is an exception, a monstrosity, within the general social condition.

The little aristocratic societies formed by certain industries in the midst of the vast democracy of our day contain, as did the great aristocratic societies of former days, some very opulent men and a multitude of wretchedly poor ones.

These poor men have few means of escaping from their condition and becoming rich, but the rich are constantly becoming poor or retiring from business when they have realized their profits. Hence the elements forming the poor class are more or less fixed, but that is not true of those forming the rich class. To be exact, although there are rich men, a class of the rich does not exist at all, for these rich men have neither corporate spirit nor objects in common, neither common traditions nor hopes. There are limbs, then, but no body.

Not only is there no solidarity among the rich, but one may say that there is no true link between rich and poor.

They are not forever fixed, one close to the other; at any moment interest, which brought them together, can pull them apart. The workman is dependent on masters in general, but not on a particular master. These two men see each other at the factory but do not know each other otherwise, and though there is one point of contact, in all other respects they stand far apart. The industrialist only asks the workman for his work, and the latter only asks him for his pay. The one contracts no obligation to protect, nor the other to defend, and they are not linked in any permanent fashion either by custom or by duty.

A business aristocracy seldom lives among the manufacturing population which it directs; its object is not to rule the latter but to make use of it.

An aristocracy so constituted cannot have a great hold over its employees, and even if it does for a moment hold them, they will soon escape. It does not know its own mind and cannot act.

The territorial aristocracy of past ages was obliged by law, or thought itself obliged by custom, to come to the help of its servants and relieve their distress. But the industrial aristocracy of our day, when it has impoverished and brutalized the men it uses, abandons them in time of crisis to public charity to feed them. This is the natural result of what has been said before. Between workman and master there are frequent relations but no true association.

I think that, generally speaking, the manufacturing aristocracy which we see rising before our eyes is one of the hardest that have appeared on earth. But at the same time, it is one of the most restrained and least dangerous.

In any event, the friends of democracy should keep their eyes anxiously fixed in that direction. For if ever again permanent inequality of conditions and aristocracy make their way into the world, it will have been by that door that they entered.

Interpretive Questions

1. Why does Tocqueville say that the worker has been assigned to a certain "position in society" instead of to a certain job?

2. Why does Tocqueville say industrial theory is stronger than morality or law?

3. According to Tocqueville, why does a democracy breed its own aristocracy?

4. Why isn't Tocqueville certain that an industrial aristocracy presents a threat to democracy?

5. Why do all the benefits from the division of labor accrue to the industrial aristocracy?

ERPRETA
EVALUATION
TION FAC
FACT IN
ON EVALU
UATION FA
RETATIO
FACT INT
VALUATION
NTERPRE
CT EVALUA
RETATION
ATION FAC
ERPRETA
FACT EVA
ON FACT
ATION INT
FACT EVA
ERPRETA
ALUATION
RETATIO
FACT INT
NTERPRE
ATION INT
ETATIONI

Questions of Fact, Interpretation, and Evaluation

Three kinds of questions are asked about a selection in shared inquiry: questions of fact, questions of interpretation, and questions of evaluation.

Questions of fact ask you to recall something in the selection, using your own words or the words of the author. A question of fact has only one correct answer.

Questions of interpretation ask you to offer your opinion about what the selection means. Unlike a question of fact, a question of interpretation usually has more than one correct answer.

Questions of evaluation ask you whether you agree or disagree with what the author said or whether something in the selection has application to your own life. You support your answer to a question of evaluation by talking about your own values or your own experiences rather than about the selection itself.

Since interpreting literature is the main purpose of the Great Books program, discussion focuses on questions of interpretation. Factual questions are used to bring out evidence in support of interpretations. Questions of evaluation are asked only after the meaning of a selection has been clarified through discussion.

This exercise will give you practice in distinguishing questions of fact, interpretation, and evaluation. In the blank before each of the following questions, write (F) if the question is FACTUAL, (I) if it is INTERPRETIVE, or (E) if it is EVALUATIVE. If you are in doubt about how to classify any question, refer to the selection.

_____ 1. Why does Tocqueville call the workman's trade a "chosen calling"?

_____ 2. What are the two axioms of industrial science?

_____ 3. Why does the development of industry increase the mental capacity of the master?

_____ 4. Do the people who run big business in America pose a threat to democracy?

_____ 5. Does Tocqueville assume most workers have the intelligence to do more than specialized manual labor?

_____ 6. Do the rich now form a class in our society?

_____ 7. Who is responsible for the plight of the workman?

_____ 8. What is the difference between an artisan and a workman?

_____ 9. Does Tocqueville think the degrading of the working class is inevitable?

_____ 10. Are Tocqueville's two axioms of industrial science true?

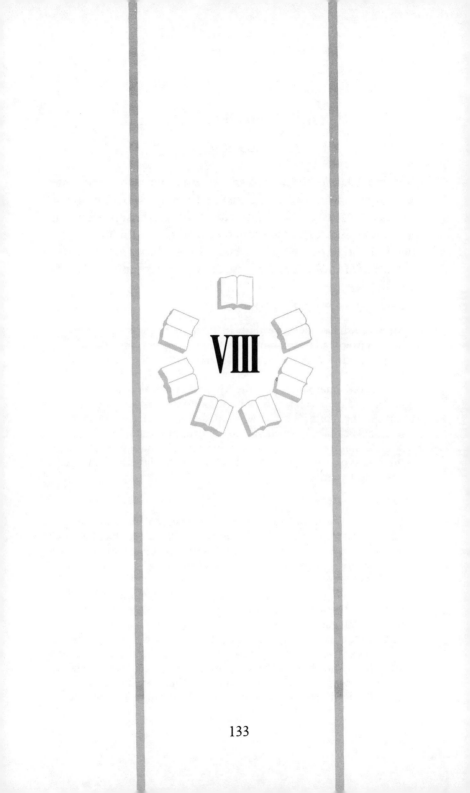

VIII

By and About Claude Bernard

(1813–1878)

When Claude Bernard died, he was given the first state funeral ever accorded a scientist in France. He was honored for his many discoveries in medicine, for establishing general physiology as a respected branch of medicine, and for making medicine an experimental science. In *An Introduction to Experimental Medicine,* Bernard discusses the philosophy and practice of science.

On the experimental method:

> Men who have excessive faith in their theories or ideas are not only ill prepared for making discoveries; they also make very poor observations. Of necessity, they observe with a preconceived idea, and when they devise an experiment, they can see, in its results, only a confirmation of their theory. In this way they distort observation and often neglect very important facts because they do not further their aim. This is what made us say elsewhere that we must never make experiments to confirm our ideas, but simply to control them; which means, in other terms, that one must accept the results of experiments as they come, with all their unexpectedness and irregularity.

On facts in science:

> By simply noting facts, we can never succeed in establishing a science. Pile up facts or observations as we may, we shall be none the wiser. To learn, we must necessarily reason about what we have observed, compare the facts and judge them by other facts used as controls.
>
> We usually give the name of discovery to recognition of a new fact, but I think that the idea connected with the discovered fact is what really constitutes the discovery. Facts are neither great nor small in themselves. A great discovery is a fact whose appearance in science gives rise to shining ideas, whose light dispels many obscurities and shows us new paths. There are other facts which, though new, teach us but little; they are therefore small discoveries. Finally, there are new facts which, though well observed,

teach nothing to anyone; they remain, for the moment, detached and sterile in science; they are what we may call raw facts or crude facts.

On discovery:

It has often been said that, to make discoveries, one must be ignorant. This opinion, mistaken in itself, nevertheless conceals a truth. It means that it is better to know nothing than to keep in mind fixed ideas based on theories whose confirmation we constantly seek, neglecting meanwhile everything that fails to agree with them.

Medical science was in its infancy when Claude Bernard's Introduction to the Study of Experimental Medicine *was published in 1865. Bernard's aim was to establish medicine as an exact science, comparable to chemistry and physics, by showing that the experimental method can be applied to living creatures as well as to inorganic matter. The scientist in any field, he said, must obtain accurate facts through rigorous investigation, then organize those facts by means of experimental reasoning in order to discover the laws of nature. Bernard continually stresses that scientific truth is necessarily rooted in the details of experimental investigation. The principles of such investigation are the subject of the first half of* Experimental Medicine. *In the second half, these principles are applied to case studies drawn from the author's own work. In our selection, Bernard declares that the scientist cannot conduct experiments without preconceived ideas, yet he insists that those ideas must not be permitted to distort the scientist's observations, whether in nature or in the laboratory.*

Observation
and Experiment

Claude Bernard

In Experimental Reasoning, Experimenters
Are Not Separate from Observers

Men of science who mean to embrace the principles of the experimental method as a whole, must fulfill two classes of conditions and must possess two qualities of mind which are indispensable if they are to reach their goal and succeed in the discovery of truth. First, they must have ideas which they submit to the control of facts; but at the same time they must make sure that the facts which serve as starting point or as control for the idea are correct and well established; they must be at once observers and experimenters.

Observers . . . purely and simply note the phenomena before their eyes. They must be anxious only to forearm themselves against errors of observation which might make them incompletely see or poorly define a phenomenon. To this end they use every instrument which may help make their observations more complete. Observers, then, must be photographers of phenomena; their observations must accurately represent

---

*A selection from *An Introduction to the Study of Experimental Medicine*.

nature. We must observe without any preconceived idea; the observer's mind must be passive, that is, must hold its peace; it listens to nature and writes at nature's dictation.

But when a fact is once noted and a phenomenon well observed, reasoning intervenes, and the experimenter steps forward to interpret the phenomenon.

An experimenter . . . is a man inspired by a more or less probable but anticipated interpretation of observed phenomena, to devise experiments which, in the logical order of his anticipations, shall bring results serving as controls for his hypothesis or preconceived idea. To do this, an experimenter reflects, tries out, gropes, compares, contrives, so as to find the experimental conditions best suited to gain the end which he sets before him. Of necessity we experiment with a preconceived idea. An experimenter's mind must be active, i.e., must question nature, and put all manner of queries to it according to the various hypotheses which suggest themselves.

But when the conditions of an experiment are once established and worked up according to the mind's preconceived idea, an induced or premeditated observation will, as we said, result. Phenomena then appear which the experimenter has caused, but which must now be noted, so as to learn next how to use them to control the experimental idea which brought them to birth. Now, from the moment when the result of an experiment appears, the experimenter is confronted with a real observation which he has induced and must note, like any other observation, without any preconceived idea. The experimenter must now disappear or rather change himself instantly into an observer; and it is only after he has noted the results of the experiment exactly, like those of an ordinary observation, that his mind will come back, to reason, compare and decide whether his experimental hypothesis is verified or disproved by these very results. To maintain the comparison suggested above, I may say that our experimenter puts questions to nature; but that, as soon as she speaks, he must hold his peace; he must note her answer, hear her out and in every case accept her decision. It has been said that the experimenter must force nature to unveil herself. Yes, the experimenter doubtless forces nature to unveil herself by attacking her with all manner of questions; he must never answer for her nor listen partially to her answers by taking, from the results of an experiment, only those which support or confirm his hypothesis. . . . An experimenter, who clings to his preconceived idea and notes the results of his experiment only from this point of view, falls inevitably into error, because he fails to note what he has not foreseen and so makes a partial observation. An experimenter must not hold to his idea, except as a means of inviting an answer from nature. But he must submit his idea to nature and be ready to abandon, to alter or to supplant it, in accordance with what he learns from observing the phenomena which he has induced.

Two operations must therefore be considered in any experiment. The first consists in premeditating and bringing to pass the conditions of the experiment; the second consists in noting the results of the experiment. It is impossible to devise an experiment without a preconceived idea; devising an experiment, we said, is putting a question; we never conceive a question without an idea which invites an answer. I consider it, therefore, an absolute principle that experiments must always be devised in view of a preconceived idea, no matter if the idea be not very clear nor very well defined. As for noting the results of the experiment, which is itself only an induced observation, I posit it similarly as a principle that we must here, as always, observe without a preconceived idea.

In the experimenter, we might also differentiate and separate the man who preconceives and devises an experiment from the man who carries it out or notes its results. In the former, it is the scientific investigator's mind that acts; in the latter, it is the senses that observe and note. What I am setting forth is most strikingly proved in the case of François Huber. Though blind, this great naturalist left us admirable experiments which he conceived and afterward had carried out by his serving man, who, for his part, had not a single scientific idea. So Huber was the directing mind that devised the experiment; but he was forced to borrow another's senses. The serving man stood for the passive senses, obedient to the mind in carrying out an experiment devised in the light of a preconceived idea.

People who condemn the use of hypotheses and of preconceived ideas in the experimental method make the mistake of confusing invention of an experiment with noting its results. We may truly say that the results of an experiment must be noted by a mind stripped of hypotheses and preconceived ideas. But we must beware of proscribing the use of hypotheses and of ideas when devising experiments or imagining means of observation. On the contrary . . . we must give free rein to our imagination; the idea is the essence of all reasoning and all invention. All progress depends on that. It cannot be smothered or driven away on the pretense that it may do harm; it must only be regulated and given a criterion, which is quite another matter.

The true scientist is one whose work includes both experimental theory and experimental practice. (1) He notes a fact; (2) apropos of this fact, an idea is born in his mind; (3) in the light of this idea, he reasons, devises an experiment, imagines and brings to pass its material conditions; (4) from this experiment, new phenomena result which must be observed, and so on and so forth. The mind of a scientist is always placed, as it were, between two observations: one which serves as starting point for reasoning, and the other which serves as conclusion.

To make myself clearer, I have endeavored to separate the different operations of experimental reasoning. But when it all takes place at the same time in the head of a scientist, abandoning himself to investigation in a science as vague as medicine still is, then the results of observation are so entangled with the bases of experiment that it would be alike impossible and useless to try to dissociate, from their inextricable mingling, each one of these terms. It is enough to remember the principle that an a priori idea, or better, an hypothesis, is a stimulus to experiment, and that we must let ourselves go with it freely, provided that we observe the results of our experiment rigorously and fully. If an hypothesis is not verified and disappears, the facts which it has enabled us to find are none the less acquired as indestructible materials for science.

Observers and experimenters, then, correspond to different phases of experimental research. The observer does not reason, he notes; the experimenter, on the other hand, reasons and grounds himself on acquired facts, to imagine and induce rationally other facts. But though in theory and abstractly we may differentiate observers from experimenters, it seems impossible to separate them in practice, since we see that one and the same investigator, perforce, is alternately observer and experimenter.

Things happen constantly, indeed, in this way when a single man of science discovers and explains a whole scientific question unaided. But it more often happens in the evolution of science, that different parts of experimental reasoning are shared by several men. Some of these, both in medicine and in natural history, merely gather and assemble observations; others manage to formulate more or less ingenious and more or less probable hypotheses based on these observations; then others come in to create conditions favoring the birth of an experiment to control these hypotheses; finally others apply themselves more especially to generalizing and systematizing the results obtained by the different observers and experimenters. This parceling out of the experimental domain is useful, because each one of its various parts is all the better cultivated. In fact we can easily conceive that, in certain sciences, the means of observation and experimentation are such specialized instruments that their management and use require a certain manual dexterity or the sharpening of certain senses. But while I accept specialization in the practice, I reject it utterly in the theory of science. I believe, indeed, that making generalization one's specialty is anti-philosophic and anti-scientific, in spite of what has been proclaimed by a modern philosophic school which piques itself on its scientific basis.

Experimental science, however, cannot advance on a single side of the method taken separately; it goes ahead only by the union of all parts of the method converging toward a common goal. Men who gather observations are useful only because their observations are afterward introduced into experimental reasoning; in other words, endless accumulation of observations leads nowhere. Men, who formulate hypotheses apropos of observations gathered by others, are useful only in so far as men seek to verify these hypotheses by experimenting; else these hypotheses, unverified or unverifiable by experiment, would engender nothing but systems and would bring us back to scholasticism. Men who experiment, despite all their dexterity, cannot solve problems unless they are inspired by a fortunate hypothesis based on accurate and well-made observations. Finally, men who generalize can make lasting theories only in so far as they themselves learn all the scientific details that these theories are intended to represent. Scientific generalization must proceed from particular facts to principles; and principles are the more stable as they rest on deeper details, just as a stake is the firmer, the farther it is driven into the ground.

We see, then, that the elements of the scientific method are interrelated. Facts are necessary materials; but their working up by experimental reasoning, i.e., by theory, is what establishes and really builds up science. Ideas, given form by facts, embody science. A scientific hypothesis is merely a scientific idea, preconceived or previsioned. A theory is merely a scientific idea controlled by experiment. Reasoning merely gives a form to our ideas, so that everything, first and last, leads back to an idea. The idea is what establishes, as we shall see, the starting point or the *primum movens* of all scientific reasoning, and it is also the goal in the mind's aspiration toward the unknown.

Interpretive Questions

1. For Bernard, does scientific investigation begin with an idea or with a fact?

2. Is it desirable for the experimenter and the observer to be different people?

3. Why does formulating ideas in science require both reasoning and imagination?

4. According to Bernard, why can't we learn from nature just by observing?

5. What does Bernard mean when he says "we never conceive a question without an idea which invites an answer"?

IX

By and About Flannery O'Connor

(1925–1964)

The fictional world of Flannery O'Connor, a native southerner and a devout Catholic, often appears to be populated solely by grotesque, freakish characters engaged in horrifyingly violent action. Yet she always insisted that her view of the world was positive, both Christian and comic. Consequently, she was often called on to explain the vision underlying her fiction.

On the uses of exaggeration and the grotesque:

> When you can assume that your audience holds the same beliefs you do, you can relax a little and use more normal means of talking to it; when you have to assume that it does not, then you have to make your vision apparent by shock—to the hard of hearing you shout, and for the almost-blind you draw large and startling figures.

On violence:

> We hear many complaints about the prevalence of violence in modern fiction, and it is always assumed that this violence is a bad thing and meant to be an end in itself. With the serious writer, violence is never an end in itself. It is the extreme situation that best reveals what we are essentially, and I believe these are times when writers are more interested in what we are essentially than in the tenor of our daily lives. . . . [T]he man in the violent situation reveals those qualities least dispensable in his personality, those qualities which are all he will have to take into eternity with him.

O'Connor gave such explanations with a tone of forced patience, and she felt compelled to warn her audience not to try to substitute secondary statements about a story's meaning for the primary, direct experience of reading the story itself:

When you can state the theme of a story, when you can separate it from the story itself, then you can be sure the story is not a very good one. The meaning of a story has to be embodied in it, has to be made concrete in it. A story is a way to say something that can't be said any other way, and it takes every word in the story to say what the meaning is. You tell a story because a statement would be inadequate. When anybody asks what a story is about, the only proper thing is to tell him to read the story. The meaning of fiction is not abstract meaning but experienced meaning, and the purpose of making statements about the meaning of a story is only to help you to experience that meaning more fully.

Everything That Rises Must Converge

Flannery O'Connor

Her doctor had told Julian's mother that she must lose twenty pounds on account of her blood pressure, so on Wednesday nights Julian had to take her downtown on the bus for a reducing class at the Y. The reducing class was designed for working girls over fifty, who weighed from 165 to 200 pounds. His mother was one of the slimmer ones, but she said ladies did not tell their age or weight. She would not ride the buses by herself at night since they had been integrated, and because the reducing class was one of her few pleasures, necessary for her health, and *free*, she said Julian could at least put himself out to take her, considering all she did for him. Julian did not like to consider all she did for him, but every Wednesday night he braced himself and took her.

She was almost ready to go, standing before the hall mirror, putting on her hat, while he, his hands behind him, appeared pinned to the door frame, waiting like Saint Sebastian for the arrows to begin piercing him. That hat was new and had cost her seven dollars and a half. She kept saying, "Maybe I shouldn't have paid that for it. No, I shouldn't have. I'll take it off and return it tomorrow. I shouldn't have bought it."

Julian raised his eyes to heaven. "Yes, you should have bought it," he said. "Put it on and let's go." It was a hideous hat. A purple velvet flap came down on one side of it and stood up on the other; the rest of it was green and looked like a cushion with the stuffing out. He decided it was less comical than jaunty and pathetic. Everything that gave her pleasure was small and depressed him.

She lifted the hat one more time and set it down slowly on top of her head. Two wings of gray hair protruded on either side of her florid face, but her eyes, sky-blue, were as innocent and untouched by experience as they must have been when she was ten. Were it not that she was a widow who had struggled fiercely to feed and clothe and put him through school and who was supporting him still, "until he got on his feet," she might have been a little girl that he had to take to town.

"It's all right, it's all right," he said. "Let's go." He opened the door himself and started down the walk to get her going. The sky was a dying violet and the houses stood out darkly against it, bulbous liver-colored monstrosities of a uniform ugliness though no two were alike. Since this had been a fashionable neighborhood forty years ago, his mother persisted in thinking they did well to have an apartment in it. Each house had a narrow collar of dirt around it in which sat, usually, a grubby child. Julian walked with his hands in his pockets, his head down and thrust forward and his eyes glazed with the determination to make himself completely numb during the time he would be sacrificed to her pleasure.

The door closed and he turned to find the dumpy figure, surmounted by the atrocious hat, coming toward him. "Well," she said, "you only live once and paying a little more for it, I at least won't meet myself coming and going."

"Some day I'll start making money," Julian said gloomily— he knew he never would—"and you can have one of those jokes whenever you take the fit." But first they would move. He visualized a place where the nearest neighbors would be three miles away on either side.

"I think you're doing fine," she said, drawing on her gloves. "You've only been out of school a year. Rome wasn't built in a day."

She was one of the few members of the Y reducing class who arrived in hat and gloves and who had a son who had been to college. "It takes time," she said, "and the world is in such a mess. This hat looked better on me than any of the others, though when she brought it out I said, 'Take that thing back. I wouldn't have it on my head,' and she said, 'Now wait till you see it on,' and when she put it on me, I said, 'We-ull,' and she said, 'If you ask me, that hat does something for you and you do something for the hat, and besides,' she said, 'with that hat, you won't meet yourself coming and going.' "

Julian thought he could have stood his lot better if she had been selfish, if she had been an old hag who drank and screamed at him. He walked along, saturated in depression, as if in the midst of his martyrdom he had lost his faith. Catching sight of his long, hopeless, irritated face, she stopped suddenly with a grief-stricken look, and pulled back on his arm. "Wait on me," she said, "I'm going back to the house and take this thing off and tomorrow I'm going to return it. I was out of my head. I can pay the gas bill with the seven-fifty."

He caught her arm in a vicious grip. "You are not going to take it back," he said. "I like it."

"Well," she said, "I don't think I ought . . ."

"Shut up and enjoy it," he muttered, more depressed than ever.

"With the world in the mess it's in," she said, "it's a wonder we can enjoy anything. I tell you, the bottom rail is on the top." Julian sighed.

"Of course," she said, "if you know who you are, you can go anywhere." She said this every time he took her to the reducing class. "Most of them in it are not our kind of people," she said, "but I can be gracious to anybody. I know who I am."

"They don't give a damn for your graciousness," Julian said savagely. "Knowing who you are is good for one generation only. You haven't the foggiest idea where you stand now or who you are."

She stopped and allowed her eyes to flash at him. "I most certainly do know who I am," she said, "and if you don't know who you are, I'm ashamed of you."

"Oh hell," Julian said.

"Your great-grandfather was a former governor of this state," she said. "Your grandfather was a prosperous landowner. Your grandmother was a Godhigh."

"Will you look around you," he said tensely, "and see where you are now?" and he swept his arm jerkily out to indicate the neighborhood, which the growing darkness at least made less dingy.

"You remain what you are," she said. "Your great-grandfather had a plantation and two hundred slaves."

"There are no more slaves," he said irritably.

"They were better off when they were," she said. He groaned to see that she was off on that topic. She rolled onto it every few days like a train on an open track. He knew every stop, every junction, every swamp along the way, and knew the exact point at which her conclusion would roll majestically into the station: "It's ridiculous. It's simply not realistic. They should rise, yes, but on their own side of the fence."

"Let's skip it," Julian said.

"The ones I feel sorry for," she said, "are the ones that are half white. They're tragic."

"Will you skip it?"

"Suppose we were half white. We would certainly have mixed feelings."

"I have mixed feelings now," he groaned.

"Well let's talk about something pleasant," she said. "I remember going to Grandpa's when I was a little girl. Then the house had double stairways that went up to what was really the second floor—all the cooking was done on the first. I used to like to stay down in the kitchen on account of the way the walls smelled. I would sit with my nose pressed against the plaster and take deep breaths. Actually the place belonged to the Godhighs but your grandfather Chestny paid the mortgage and saved it for them. They were in reduced circumstances," she said, "but reduced or not, they never forgot who they were."

"Doubtless that decayed mansion reminded them," Julian muttered. He never spoke of it without contempt or thought of it without longing. He had seen it once when he was a child before it had been sold. The double stairways had rotted and been torn down. Negroes were living in it. But it remained in his mind as his mother had known it. It appeared in his dreams regularly. He would stand on the wide porch, listening to the rustle of oak leaves, then wander through the high-ceilinged hall into the parlor that opened onto it and gaze at the worn rugs and faded draperies. It occurred to him that it was he, not she, who could have appreciated it. He preferred its threadbare elegance to anything he could name and it was because of it that all the neighborhoods they had lived in had been a torment to him—whereas she had hardly known the difference. She called her insensitivity "being adjustable."

"And I remember the old darky who was my nurse, Caroline. There was no better person in the world. I've always had a great respect for my colored friends," she said. "I'd do anything in the world for them and they'd . . ."

"Will you for God's sake get off that subject?" Julian said. When he got on a bus by himself, he made it a point to sit down beside a Negro, in reparation as it were for his mother's sins.

"You're mighty touchy tonight," she said. "Do you feel all right?"

"Yes I feel all right," he said. "Now lay off."

She pursed her lips. "Well, you certainly are in a vile humor," she observed. "I just won't speak to you at all."

They had reached the bus stop. There was no bus in sight and Julian, his hands still jammed in his pockets and his head thrust forward, scowled down the empty street. The frustration of having to wait on the bus as well as ride on it began to creep up his neck like a hot hand. The presence of his mother was borne in upon him as she gave a pained sigh. He looked at her bleakly. She was holding herself very erect under the preposterous hat, wearing it like a banner of her imaginary dignity. There was in him an evil urge to break her spirit. He suddenly unloosened his tie and pulled it off and put it in his pocket.

She stiffened. "Why must you look like *that* when you take me to town?" she said. "Why must you deliberately embarrass me?"

"If you'll never learn where you are," he said, "you can at least learn where I am."

"You look like a—thug," she said.

"Then I must be one," he murmured.

"I'll just go home," she said. "I will not bother you. If you can't do a little thing like that for me . . ."

Rolling his eyes upward, he put his tie back on. "Restored to my class," he muttered. He thrust his face toward her and hissed, "True culture is in the mind, the *mind*," he said, and tapped his head, "the mind."

"It's in the heart," she said, "and in how you do things and how you do things is because of who you *are*."

"Nobody in the damn bus cares who you are."

"I care who I am," she said icily.

The lighted bus appeared on top of the next hill and as it approached, they moved out into the street to meet it. He put his hand under her elbow and hoisted her up on the creaking step. She entered with a little smile, as if she were going into a drawing room where everyone had been waiting for her. While he put in the tokens, she sat down on one of the broad front seats for three which faced the aisle. A thin woman with protruding teeth and long yellow hair was sitting on the end of it. His mother moved up beside her and left room for Julian beside herself. He sat down and looked at the floor across the aisle where a pair of thin feet in red and white canvas sandals were planted.

His mother immediately began a general conversation meant to attract anyone who felt like talking. "Can it get any hotter?" she said and removed from her purse a folding fan, black with a Japanese scene on it, which she began to flutter before her.

"I reckon it might could," the woman with the protruding teeth said, "but I know for a fact my apartment couldn't get no hotter."

"It must get the afternoon sun," his mother said. She sat forward and looked up and down the bus. It was half filled. Everybody was white. "I see we have the bus to ourselves," she said. Julian cringed.

"For a change," said the woman across the aisle, the owner of the red and white canvas sandals. "I come on one the other day and they were thick as fleas—up front and all through."

"The world is in a mess everywhere," his mother said. "I don't know how we've let it get in this fix."

"What gets my goat is all those boys from good families

stealing automobile tires," the woman with the protruding teeth said. "I told my boy, I said you may not be rich but you been raised right and if I ever catch you in any such mess, they can send you on to the reformatory. Be exactly where you belong."

"Training tells," his mother said. "Is your boy in high school?"

"Ninth grade," the woman said.

"My son just finished college last year. He wants to write but he's selling typewriters until he gets started," his mother said.

The woman leaned forward and peered at Julian. He threw her such a malevolent look that she subsided against the seat. On the floor across the aisle there was an abandoned newspaper. He got up and got it and opened it out in front of him. His mother discreetly continued the conversation in a lower tone but the woman across the aisle said in a loud voice, "Well that's nice. Selling typewriters is close to writing. He can go right from one to the other."

"I tell him," his mother said, "that Rome wasn't built in a day."

Behind the newspaper Julian was withdrawing into the inner compartment of his mind where he spent most of his time. This was a kind of mental bubble in which he established himself when he could not bear to be a part of what was going on around him. From it he could see out and judge but in it he was safe from any kind of penetration from without. It was the only place where he felt free of the general idiocy of his fellows. His mother had never entered it but from it he could see her with absolute clarity.

The old lady was clever enough and he thought that if she had started from any of the right premises, more might have been expected of her. She lived according to the laws of her own fantasy world, outside of which he had never seen her set foot. The law of it was to sacrifice herself for him after she had first created the necessity to do so by making a mess of things. If he had permitted her sacrifices, it was only because her lack of foresight had made them necessary. All of her life had been a struggle to act like a Chestny without the Chestny goods, and to give him everything she thought a Chestny ought to have; but since, she said, it was fun to struggle, why complain? And when you had won, as she had won, what fun to look back on the hard times! He could not forgive her that she had enjoyed the struggle and that she thought *she* had won.

What she meant when she said she had won was that she had brought him up successfully and had sent him to college and that he had turned out so well—good looking (her teeth had gone unfilled so that his could be straightened), intelligent (he realized he was too intelligent to be a success), and with a future ahead of him (there was of course no future ahead of him). She excused his gloominess on the grounds that he was still growing up and his radical ideas on his lack of practical experience. She said he didn't yet know a thing about "life," that he hadn't even entered the real world—when already he was as disenchanted with it as a man of fifty.

The further irony of all this was that in spite of her, he had turned out so well. In spite of going to only a third-rate college, he had, on his own initiative, come out with a first-rate education; in spite of growing up dominated by a small mind, he had ended up with a large one; in spite of all her foolish views, he was free of prejudice and unafraid to face facts. Most miraculous of all, instead of being blinded by love for her as she was for him, he had cut himself emotionally free of her and could see her with complete objectivity. He was not dominated by his mother.

The bus stopped with a sudden jerk and shook him from his meditation. A woman from the back lurched forward with little steps and barely escaped falling in his newspaper as she righted herself. She got off and a large Negro got on. Julian kept his paper lowered to watch. It gave him a certain satisfaction to see injustice in daily operation. It confirmed his view that with a few exceptions there was no one worth knowing within a radius of three hundred miles. The Negro was well dressed and carried a briefcase. He looked around and then sat down on the other end of the seat where the woman with the red and white canvas sandals was sitting. He immediately unfolded a newspaper and obscured himself behind it. Julian's mother's elbow at once prodded insistently into his ribs. "Now you see why I won't ride on these buses by myself," she whispered.

The woman with the red and white canvas sandals had risen at the same time the Negro sat down and had gone further back in the bus and taken the seat of the woman who had got off. His mother leaned forward and cast her an approving look.

Julian rose, crossed the aisle, and sat down in the place of the woman with the canvas sandals. From this position, he looked serenely across at his mother. Her face had turned an angry red. He stared at her, making his eyes the eyes of a stranger. He felt his tension suddenly lift as if he had openly declared war on her.

He would have liked to get in conversation with the Negro and to talk with him about art or politics or any subject that would be above the comprehension of those around them, but the man remained entrenched behind his paper. He was either ignoring the change of seating or had never noticed it. There was no way for Julian to convey his sympathy.

His mother kept her eyes fixed reproachfully on his face. The woman with the protruding teeth was looking at him avidly as if he were a type of monster new to her.

"Do you have a light?" he asked the Negro.

Without looking away from his paper, the man reached in his pocket and handed him a packet of matches.

"Thanks," Julian said. For a moment he held the matches foolishly. A NO SMOKING sign looked down upon him from over the door. This alone would not have deterred him; he had no cigarettes. He had quit smoking some months before because he could not afford it. "Sorry," he muttered and handed back the matches. The Negro lowered the paper and gave him an annoyed look. He took the matches and raised the paper again.

His mother continued to gaze at him but she did not take advantage of his momentary discomfort. Her eyes retained their battered look. Her face seemed to be unnaturally red, as if her blood pressure had risen. Julian allowed no glimmer of sympathy to show on his face. Having got the advantage, he wanted desperately to keep it and carry it through. He would have liked to teach her a lesson that would last her a while, but there seemed no way to continue the point. The Negro refused to come out from behind his paper.

Julian folded his arms and looked stolidly before him, facing her but as if he did not see her, as if he had ceased to recognize her existence. He visualized a scene in which, the bus having reached their stop, he would remain in his seat and when she said, "Aren't you going to get off?" he would look at her as at a stranger who had rashly addressed him. The corner they got off on was usually deserted, but it was well lighted and it would not hurt her to walk by herself the four blocks to the Y. He decided to wait until the time came and then decide whether or not he would let her get off by herself. He would have to be at the Y at ten to bring her back, but he could leave her wondering if he was going to show up. There was no reason for her to think she could always depend on him.

He retired again into the high-ceilinged room sparsely settled with large pieces of antique furniture. His soul expanded momentarily but then he became aware of his mother across from him and the vision shriveled. He studied her coldly. Her feet in little pumps dangled like a child's and did not quite reach the floor. She was training on him an exaggerated look of reproach. He felt completely detached from her. At that moment he could with pleasure have slapped her as he would have slapped a particularly obnoxious child in his charge.

He began to imagine various unlikely ways by which he could teach her a lesson. He might make friends with some distinguished Negro professor or lawyer and bring him home to spend the evening. He would be entirely justified but her blood pressure would rise to 300. He could not push her to the extent of making her have a stroke, and moreover, he had never been successful at making any Negro friends. He had tried to strike up an acquaintance on the bus with some of the better types, with ones that looked like professors or ministers or lawyers. One morning he had sat down next to a distinguished-looking dark brown man who had answered his questions with a sonorous solemnity but who had turned out to be an undertaker. Another day he had sat down beside a cigar-smoking Negro with a diamond ring on his finger, but after a few stilted pleasantries, the Negro had rung the buzzer and risen, slipping two lottery tickets into Julian's hand as he climbed over him to leave.

He imagined his mother lying desperately ill and his being able to secure only a Negro doctor for her. He toyed with that idea for a few minutes and then dropped it for a momentary vision of himself participating as a sympathizer in a sit-in demonstration. This was possible but he did not linger with it. Instead, he approached the ultimate horror. He brought home a beautiful suspiciously Negroid woman. Prepare yourself, he said. There is nothing you can do about it. This is the woman I've chosen. She's intelligent, dignified, even good, and she's suffered and she hasn't thought it *fun*. Now persecute us, go ahead and persecute us. Drive her out of here, but remember, you're driving me too. His eyes were narrowed and through the indignation he had generated, he saw his mother across the aisle, purple-faced, shrunken to the dwarf-like proportions of her moral nature, sitting like a mummy beneath the ridiculous banner of her hat.

He was tilted out of his fantasy again as the bus stopped. The door opened with a sucking hiss and out of the dark a large, gaily dressed, sullen-looking colored woman got on with a little boy. The child, who might have been four, had on a short plaid suit and a Tyrolean hat with a blue feather in it. Julian hoped that he would sit down beside him and that the woman would push in beside his mother. He could think of no better arrangement.

As she waited for her tokens, the woman was surveying the seating possibilities—he hoped with the idea of sitting where she was least wanted. There was something familiar-looking about her but Julian could not place what it was. She was a giant of a woman. Her face was set not only to meet opposition but to seek it out. The downward tilt of her large lower lip was like a warning sign: DON'T TAMPER WITH ME. Her bulging figure was encased in a green crepe dress and her feet overflowed in red shoes. She had on a hideous hat. A purple velvet flap came down on one side of it and stood up on the other; the rest of it was green and looked like a cushion with the stuffing out. She carried a mammoth red pocketbook that bulged throughout as if it were stuffed with rocks.

To Julian's disappointment, the little boy climbed up on the empty seat beside his mother. His mother lumped all children, black and white, into the common category, "cute," and she thought little Negroes were on the whole cuter than little white children. She smiled at the little boy as he climbed on the seat.

Meanwhile the woman was bearing down upon the empty

seat beside Julian. To his annoyance, she squeezed herself into it. He saw his mother's face change as the woman settled herself next to him and he realized with satisfaction that this was more objectionable to her than it was to him. Her face seemed almost gray and there was a look of dull recognition in her eyes, as if suddenly she had sickened at some awful confrontation. Julian saw that it was because she and the woman had, in a sense, swapped sons. Though his mother would not realize the symbolic significance of this, she would feel it. His amusement showed plainly on his face.

The woman next to him muttered something unintelligible to herself. He was conscious of a kind of bristling next to him, muted growling like that of an angry cat. He could not see anything but the red pocketbook upright on the bulging green thighs. He visualized the woman as she had stood waiting for her tokens—the ponderous figure, rising from the red shoes upward over the solid hips, the mammoth bosom, the haughty face, to the green and purple hat.

His eyes widened.

The vision of the two hats, identical, broke upon him with the radiance of a brilliant sunrise. His face was suddenly lit with joy. He could not believe that Fate had thrust upon his mother such a lesson. He gave a loud chuckle so that she would look at him and see that he saw. She turned her eyes on him slowly. The blue in them seemed to have turned a bruised purple. For a moment he had an uncomfortable sense of her innocence, but it lasted only a second before principle rescued him. Justice entitled him to laugh. His grin hardened until it said to her as plainly as if he were saying aloud: Your punishment exactly fits your pettiness. This should teach you a permanent lesson.

Her eyes shifted to the woman. She seemed unable to bear looking at him and to find the woman preferable. He became conscious again of the bristling presence at his side. The woman was rumbling like a volcano about to become active. His mother's mouth began to twitch slightly at one corner. With a sinking heart, he saw incipient signs of recovery on her face and realized that this was going to strike her suddenly as funny and was going to be no lesson at all. She kept her eyes on the woman and an amused smile came over her face as if the woman were a monkey that had stolen her hat. The little Negro was looking up at her with large fascinated eyes. He had been trying to attract her attention for some time.

"Carver!" the woman said suddenly. "Come heah!"

When he saw that the spotlight was on him at last, Carver drew his feet up and turned himself toward Julian's mother and giggled.

"Carver!" the woman said. "You heah me? Come heah!"

Carver slid down from the seat but remained squatting with his back against the base of it, his head turned slyly around toward Julian's mother, who was smiling at him. The woman reached a hand across the aisle and snatched him to her. He righted himself and hung backwards on her knees, grinning at Julian's mother. "Isn't he cute?" Julian's mother said to the woman with the protruding teeth.

"I reckon he is," the woman said without conviction.

The Negress yanked him upright but he eased out of her grip and shot across the aisle and scrambled, giggling wildly, onto the seat beside his love.

"I think he likes me," Julian's mother said, and smiled at the woman. It was the smile she used when she was being particularly gracious to an inferior. Julian saw everything lost. The lesson had rolled off her like rain on a roof.

The woman stood up and yanked the little boy off the seat as if she were snatching him from contagion. Julian could feel the rage in her at having no weapon like his mother's smile.

She gave the child a sharp slap across his leg. He howled once and then thrust his head into her stomach and kicked his feet against her shins. "Behave," she said vehemently.

The bus stopped and the Negro who had been reading the newspaper got off. The woman moved over and set the little boy down with a thump between herself and Julian. She held him firmly by the knee. In a moment he put his hands in front of his face and peeped at Julian's mother through his fingers.

"I see yoooooooo!" she said and put her hand in front of her face and peeped at him.

The woman slapped his hand down. "Quit yo' foolishness," she said, "before I knock the living Jesus out of you!"

Julian was thankful that the next stop was theirs. He reached up and pulled the cord. The woman reached up and pulled it at the same time. Oh my God, he thought. He had the terrible intuition that when they got off the bus together, his mother would open her purse and give the little boy a nickel. The gesture would be as natural to her as breathing. The bus stopped and the woman got up and lunged to the front, dragging the child, who wished to stay on, after her. Julian and his mother got up and followed. As they neared the door, Julian tried to relieve her of her pocketbook.

"No," she murmured, "I want to give the little boy a nickel."

"No!" Julian hissed. "No!"

She smiled down at the child and opened her bag. The bus door opened and the woman picked him up by the arm and descended with him, hanging at her hip. Once in the street she set him down and shook him.

Julian's mother had to close her purse while she got down the bus step but as soon as her feet were on the ground, she opened it again and began to rummage inside. "I can't find but a penny," she whispered, "but it looks like a new one."

"Don't do it!" Julian said fiercely between his teeth. There was a streetlight on the corner and she hurried to get under it so that she could better see into her pocketbook. The woman was heading off rapidly down the street with the child still hanging backward on her hand.

"Oh little boy!" Julian's mother called and took a few quick steps and caught up with them just beyond the lamppost. "Here's a bright new penny for you," and she held out the coin, which shone bronze in the dim light.

The huge woman turned and for a moment stood, her shoulders lifted and her face frozen with frustrated rage, and stared at Julian's mother. Then all at once she seemed to explode like a piece of machinery that had been given one ounce of pressure too much. Julian saw the black fist swing out with the red pocketbook. He shut his eyes and cringed as he heard the woman shout, "He don't take nobody's pennies!" When he opened his eyes, the woman was disappearing down the street with the little boy staring wide-eyed over her shoulder. Julian's mother was sitting on the sidewalk.

"I told you not to do that," Julian said angrily. "I told you not to do that!"

He stood over her for a minute, gritting his teeth. Her legs were stretched out in front of her and her hat was on her lap. He squatted down and looked her in the face. It was totally expressionless. "You got exactly what you deserved," he said. "Now get up."

He picked up her pocketbook and put what had fallen out back in it. He picked the hat up off her lap. The penny caught his eye on the sidewalk and he picked that up and let it drop before her eyes into the purse. Then he stood up and leaned over and held his hands out to pull her up. She remained immobile. He sighed. Rising above them on either side were black apartment buildings, marked with irregular rectangles of light. At the end of the block a man came out of a door and walked off in the opposite direction. "All right," he said, "suppose somebody happens by and wants to know why you're sitting on the sidewalk?"

She took the hand and, breathing hard, pulled heavily up on it and then stood for a moment, swaying slightly as if the spots of light in the darkness were circling around her. Her eyes, shadowed and confused, finally settled on his face. He did not try to conceal his irritation. "I hope this teaches you a lesson," he said. She leaned forward and her eyes raked his face. She seemed trying to determine his identity. Then, as if she found nothing familiar about him, she started off with a headlong movement in the wrong direction.

"Aren't you going on to the Y?" he asked.

"Home," she muttered.

"Well, are we walking?"

For answer she kept going. Julian followed along, his hands behind him. He saw no reason to let the lesson she had had go without backing it up with an explanation of its meaning. She might as well be made to understand what had happened to her. "Don't think that was just an uppity Negro woman," he said. "That was the whole colored race which will no longer take your condescending pennies. That was your black double. She can wear the same hat as you, and to be sure," he added gratuitously (because he thought it was funny), "it looked better on her than it did on you. What all this means," he said, "is that the old world is gone. The old manners are obsolete and your graciousness is not worth a damn." He thought bitterly of the house that had been lost for him. "You aren't who you think you are," he said.

She continued to plow ahead, paying no attention to him. Her hair had come undone on one side. She dropped her pocketbook and took no notice. He stooped and picked it up and handed it to her but she did not take it.

"You needn't act as if the world had come to an end," he said, "because it hasn't. From now on you've got to live in a new world and face a few realities for a change. Buck up," he said, "it won't kill you."

She was breathing fast.

"Let's wait on the bus," he said.

"Home," she said thickly.

"I hate to see you behave like this," he said. "Just like a child. I should be able to expect more of you." He decided to stop where he was and make her stop and wait for a bus. "I'm not going any farther," he said, stopping. "We're going on the bus."

She continued to go on as if she had not heard him. He took a few steps and caught her arm and stopped her. He looked into her face and caught his breath. He was looking into a face he had never seen before. "Tell Grandpa to come get me," she said.

He stared, stricken.

"Tell Caroline to come get me," she said.

Stunned, he let her go and she lurched forward again, walking as if one leg were shorter than the other. A tide of darkness seemed to be sweeping her from him. "Mother!" he cried. "Darling, sweetheart, wait!" Crumpling, she fell to the pavement. He dashed forward and fell at her side, crying, "Mamma, Mamma!" He turned her over. Her face was fiercely distorted. One eye, large and staring, moved slightly to the left as if it had become unmoored. The other remained fixed on him, raked his face again, found nothing and closed.

"Wait here, wait here!" he cried and jumped up and began to run for help toward a cluster of lights he saw in the distance ahead of him. "Help, help!" he shouted, but his voice was thin, scarcely a thread of sound. The lights drifted farther away the faster he ran and his feet moved numbly as if they carried him nowhere. The tide of darkness seemed to sweep him back to her, postponing from moment to moment his entry into the world of guilt and sorrow.

Interpretive Questions

1. Why does Julian's mother become so upset that she suffers a stroke?

2. Why is the black woman enraged at her son's behavior with Julian's mother?

3. Why does O'Connor have Julian's mother and the black woman wearing the same hats?

4. Why do both Julian and his mother revert to childhood at the end of the story?

5. Why doesn't Julian get along with his mother?

Is Freud hopeful th

If the Melian
war or slavery

Are my social
imposed on me

Why does Jacob coc
has never made ?

Why does Smith su
sufficiency is not a

Why is Gavrila
oppressed by the

Who is responsible
workman in societ

Can facts be disco

Why is Julian
a success ?

Does Fry think art

By the end of t
civilized virtues

Why does a studen
knowing as knowl
specialized ?

Why does Orte
a discipline su
say the truths
by one man ?

Developing Interpretive Questions

The more you participate in Great Books
discussions, the more you will see problems of
meaning in the selections you read. Some of your
notes may already be in the form of interpretive
questions; others can be developed into questions.

Writing interpretive questions from your
notes will help you to prepare for discussion.
Remember that an interpretive question is a
question you care about that can be explored
using the text everyone has read. It has more than
one possible correct answer.

The most likely sources of interpretive questions are listed here, together with the questions one reader developed from her responses to "Everything That Rises Must Converge."

What seems important. Julian seems to disagree with his mother on almost every issue: his mother claims to know who she is, he says she doesn't; she wants to give the child a coin, he doesn't want her to; she thinks the hat is right for her, he detests it. This led to the question

Why doesn't Julian get along with his mother?

What you don't understand. The reader didn't understand why Julian acts as he does toward the black people on the bus. There is a gap between his intentions and his ability to carry them out. So the reader asked

Why are Julian's efforts to communicate with black people unsuccessful?

What you agree or disagree with. The reader disliked the attitude that Julian's mother has toward the black people in the story and wondered why she acts as she does. This led to the question

Why does Julian's mother play with the black child and try to give him a coin?

What the author seems to emphasize. The hat that Julian's mother wears at the beginning of the story is described in great detail and is a source of tension between her and Julian. Later the black woman boards the bus wearing an identical hat. The reader wanted to know why the author makes the hat an important part of the story, so she asked

Why does O'Connor have Julian's mother and the black woman wearing the same hat?

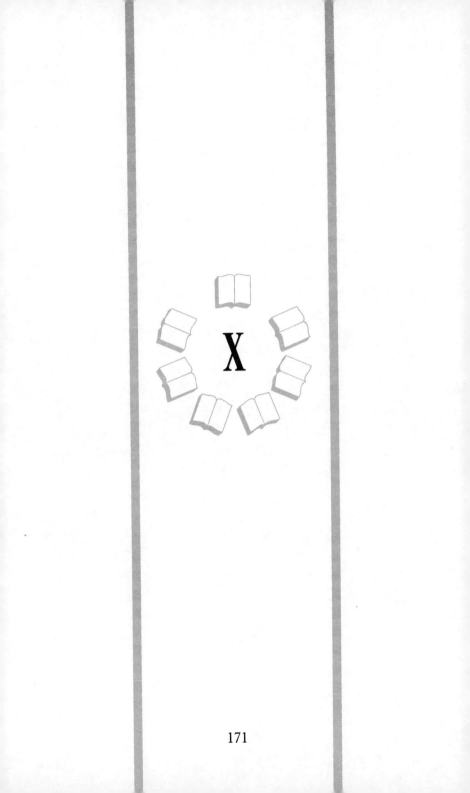

X

By and About Roger Fry

(1866–1934)

When Roger Fry left Cambridge University, he abandoned the scientific career for which he had been trained and resolved instead to devote himself to painting. He later said:

> I am the victim of perhaps quite an absurd faith—the faith, namely, that the aesthetic pursuit is as important in the long run for mankind as the search for truth.

Fry was an established connoisseur and scholar of Italian Renaissance art when he published "An Essay in Aesthetics" in 1909. The following year he jeopardized his reputation and career when he exhibited the works of Cézanne, Manet, Gauguin, Van Gogh, and Matisse for the English art community. The press described these artists as "bunglers" and "lunatics" whose work revealed "the existence of a widespread plot to destroy the whole fabric of European painting." Looking back upon this widespread and highly emotional response, Fry concluded that he had touched more than just an aesthetic chord:

> The accusation of anarchism was constantly made. From an aesthetic point of view this was, of course, the exact opposite of the truth, and I was for long puzzled to find the explanation of so paradoxical an opinion and so violent an enmity. I now see that my crime had been to strike at the vested emotional interest ... the accusation of revolutionary anarchism was due to a social rather than an aesthetic prejudice.

Toward the latter part of his career, Fry reflected on his work and the nature of his ideas:

> In my work as a critic of art I have never been a pure Impressionist, a mere recording instrument of certain sensations. I have always had some kind of aesthetic. A certain scientific curiosity and a desire for comprehension have impelled me at every stage to make generalizations, to attempt some kind of logical co-ordination of my impressions. . . . I have never believed that I knew what was the ultimate nature of art.

One of the most enduring ideas about the nature of art holds that art imitates or represents objects and actions in the world. But if art merely copies reality, why do we need it? In Vision and Design, Roger Fry answers this question by proposing a different way of understanding art. According to Fry, we live a double life. In our "actual life," objects and events arouse our emotions and demand that we respond with some appropriate action. For example, the witness of an accident may rush to help the victim or choose not to become involved. In the "imaginative life," however, no such action is possible: a person who sees a picture of the accident or recalls it from the past can do nothing about it. Art, Fry says, is the expression of this imaginative life; it converts us from actors into spectators, asking us only to feel our emotions more clearly.

An Essay in Aesthetics

Roger Fry

A certain painter, not without some reputation at the present day, once wrote a little book on the art he practises, in which he gave a definition of that art so succinct that I take it as a point of departure for this essay.

"The art of painting," says that eminent authority, "is the art of imitating solid objects upon a flat surface by means of pigments." It is delightfully simple, but prompts the question—Is that all? And, if so, what a deal of unnecessary fuss has been made about it. Now, it is useless to deny that our modern writer has some very respectable authorities behind him. Plato, indeed, gave a very similar account of the affair, and himself put the question—Is it then worth while? And, being scrupulously and relentlessly logical, he decided that it was not worth while, and proceeded to turn the artists out of his ideal republic. For all that, the world has continued obstinately to consider that painting was worth while, and though, indeed, it has

---

*A selection from *Vision and Design*.

never quite made up its mind as to what, exactly, the graphic arts did for it, it has persisted in honouring and admiring its painters.

Can we arrive at any conclusions as to the nature of the graphic arts, which will at all explain our feelings about them, which will at least put them into some kind of relation with the other arts, and not leave us in the extreme perplexity engendered by any theory of mere imitation? For, I suppose, it must be admitted that if imitation is the sole purpose of the graphic arts, it is surprising that the works of such arts are ever looked upon as more than curiosities, or ingenious toys, are ever taken seriously by grown-up people. Moreover, it will be surprising that they have no recognisable affinity with other arts, such as music or architecture, in which the imitation of actual objects is a negligible quantity.

To form such conclusions is the aim I have put before myself in this essay. Even if the results are not decisive, the inquiry may lead us to a view of the graphic arts that will not be altogether unfruitful.

I must begin with some elementary psychology, with a consideration of the nature of instincts. A great many objects in the world, when presented to our senses, put in motion a complex nervous machinery, which ends in some instinctive appropriate action. We see a wild bull in a field; quite without our conscious interference a nervous process goes on, which, unless we interfere forcibly, ends in the appropriate reaction of flight. The nervous mechanism which results in flight causes a certain state of consciousness, which we call the emotion of fear. The whole of animal life, and a great part of human life, is made up of these instinctive reactions to sensible objects, and their accompanying emotions. But man has the peculiar faculty of calling up again in his mind the echo of past experiences of this kind, of going over it again, "in imagination" as we say.

He has, therefore, the possibility of a double life; one the actual life, the other the imaginative life. Between these two lives there is this great distinction, that in the actual life the processes of natural selection have brought it about that the instinctive reaction, such, for instance, as flight from danger, shall be the important part of the whole process, and it is towards this that the man bends his whole conscious endeavour. But in the imaginative life no such action is necessary, and, therefore, the whole consciousness may be focussed upon the perceptive and the emotional aspects of the experience. In this way we get, in the imaginative life, a different set of values, and a different kind of perception.

We can get a curious side glimpse of the nature of this imaginative life from the cinematograph. This resembles actual life in almost every respect, except that what the psychologists call the conative part of our reaction to sensations, that is to say, the appropriate resultant action is cut off. If, in a cinematograph, we see a runaway horse and cart, we do not have to think either of getting out of the way or heroically interposing ourselves. The result is that in the first place we *see* the event much more clearly; see a number of quite interesting but irrelevant things, which in real life could not struggle into our consciousness, bent, as it would be, entirely upon the problem of our appropriate reaction. I remember seeing in a cinematograph the arrival of a train at a foreign station and the people descending from the carriages; there was no platform, and to my intense surprise I saw several people turn right round after reaching the ground, as though to orientate themselves; an almost ridiculous performance, which I had never noticed in all the many hundred occasions on which such a scene had passed before my eyes in real life. The fact being that at a station one is never really a spectator of events, but an actor engaged in the drama of luggage or prospective seats, and one actually sees only so much as may help to the appropriate action.

In the second place, with regard to the visions of the cinematograph, one notices that whatever emotions are aroused by them, though they are likely to be weaker than those of ordinary life, are presented more clearly to the consciousness. If the scene presented be one of an accident, our pity and horror, though weak, since we know that no one is really hurt, are felt quite purely, since they cannot, as they would in life, pass at once into actions of assistance.

A somewhat similar effect to that of the cinematograph can be obtained by watching a mirror in which a street scene is reflected. If we look at the street itself we are almost sure to adjust ourselves in some way to its actual existence. We recognise an acquaintance, and wonder why he looks so dejected this morning, or become interested in a new fashion in hats—the moment we do that the spell is broken, we are reacting to life itself in however slight a degree, but, in the mirror, it is easier to abstract ourselves completely, and look upon the changing scene as a whole. It then, at once, takes on the visionary quality, and we become true spectators, not selecting what we will see, but seeing everything equally, and thereby we come to notice a number of appearances and relations of appearances, which would have escaped our notice before, owing to that perpetual economising by selection of what impressions we will assimilate, which in life we perform by unconscious processes. The frame of the mirror, then, does to some extent turn the reflected scene from one that belongs to our actual life into one that belongs rather to the imaginative life. The frame of the mirror makes its surface into a very rudimentary work of art, since it helps us to attain to the artistic vision. For that is what, as you will already have guessed, I have been coming to all this time, namely that the work of art is intimately connected with the secondary imaginative life, which all men live to a greater or less extent.

That the graphic arts are the expression of the imaginative life rather than a copy of actual life might be guessed from observing children. Children, if left to themselves, never, I believe, copy what they see, never, as we say, "draw from nature," but express, with a delightful freedom and sincerity, the mental images which make up their own imaginative lives.

Art, then, is an expression and a stimulus of this imaginative life, which is separated from actual life by the absence of responsive action. Now this responsive action implies in actual life moral responsibility. In art we have no such moral responsibility—it presents a life freed from the binding necessities of our actual existence. . . .

. . . Art, then, is, if I am right, the chief organ of the imaginative life; it is by art that it is stimulated and controlled within us, and, as we have seen, the imaginative life is distinguished by the greater clearness of its perception, and the greater purity and freedom of its emotion.

First with regard to the greater clearness of perception. The needs of our actual life are so imperative that the sense of vision becomes highly specialised in their service. With an admirable economy we learn to see only so much as is needful for our purposes; but this is in fact very little, just enough to recognise and identify each object or person; that done, they go into an entry in our mental catalogue and are no more really seen. In actual life the normal person really only reads the labels, as it were, on the objects around him and troubles no further. Almost all the things which are useful in any way put on, more or less, this cap of invisibility. It is only when an object exists in our lives for no other purpose than to be seen that we really look at it, as for instance at a China ornament or a precious stone, and towards such even the most normal person adopts to some extent the artistic attitude of pure vision abstracted from necessity.

Now this specialisation of vision goes so far that ordinary people have almost no idea of what things really look like, so that oddly enough the one standard that popular criticism applies to painting, namely, whether it is like nature or not, is one which most people are, by the whole tenour of their lives, prevented from applying properly. The only things they have ever really *looked* at being other pictures; the moment an artist who has looked at nature brings to them a clear report of something definitely seen by him, they are wildly indignant at its untruth to nature. This has happened so constantly in our own time that there is no need to prove it. . . .

But though this clarified sense perception which we discover in the imaginative life is of great interest, and although it plays a larger part in the graphic arts than in any other, it might perhaps be doubted whether, interesting, curious, fascinating as it is, this aspect of the imaginative life would ever by itself make art of profound importance to mankind. But it is different, I think, with the emotional aspect. . . . The more poignant emotions of actual life have, I think, a kind of numbing effect analogous to the paralysing influence of fear in some animals; but even if this experience be not generally admitted, all will admit that the need for responsive action hurries us along and prevents us from ever realising fully what the emotion is that we feel, from co-ordinating it perfectly with other states. In short, the motives we actually experience are too close to us to enable us to feel them clearly. They are in a sense unintelligible. In the imaginative life, on the contrary, we can both feel the emotion and watch it. When we are really moved at the theatre we are always both on the stage and in the auditorium.

Yet another point about the emotions of the imaginative life—since they require no responsive action we can give them a new valuation. In real life we must to some extent cultivate those emotions which lead to useful action, and we are bound to appraise emotions according to the resultant action. So that, for instance, the feelings of rivalry and emulation do get an encouragement which perhaps they scarcely deserve, whereas certain feelings which appear to have a high intrinsic value get almost no stimulus in actual life. For instance, those feelings to which the name of the cosmic emotion has been somewhat unhappily given find almost no place in life, but, since they seem to belong to certain very deep springs of our nature, do become of great importance in the arts.

Morality, then, appreciates emotion by the standard of resultant action. Art appreciates emotion in and for itself.

This view of the essential importance in art of the expression of the emotions is the basis of Tolstoy's marvellously original and yet perverse and even exasperating book, *What is Art?* and I willingly confess, while disagreeing with almost all his results, how much I owe to him.

He gives an example of what he means by calling art the means of communicating emotions. He says, let us suppose a boy to have been pursued in the forest by a bear. If he returns to the village and merely states that he was pursued by a bear and escaped, that is ordinary language, the means of communicating facts or ideas; but if he describes his state first of heedlessness, then of sudden alarm and terror as the bear appears, and finally of relief when he gets away, and describes this so that his hearers share his emotions, then his description is a work of art. . . .

If, then, an object of any kind is created by man not for use, for its fitness to actual life, but as an object of art, an object subserving the imaginative life, what will its qualities be? It must in the first place be adapted to that disinterested intensity of contemplation, which we have found to be the effect of cutting off the responsive action. It must be suited to that heightened power of perception which we found to result therefrom.

And the first quality that we demand in our sensations will be order, without which our sensations will be troubled and perplexed, and the other quality will be variety, without which they will not be fully stimulated.

It may be objected that many things in nature, such as flowers, possess these two qualities of order and variety in a high degree, and these objects do undoubtedly stimulate and satisfy that clear disinterested contemplation which is characteristic of the aesthetic attitude. But in our reaction to a work of art there is something more—there is the consciousness of purpose, the consciousness of a peculiar relation of sympathy with the man who made this thing in order to arouse precisely the sensations we experience. And when we come to the higher works of art, where sensations are so arranged that they arouse in us deep emotions, this feeling of a special tie with the man who expressed them becomes very strong. We feel that he has expressed something which was latent in us all the time, but which we never realised, that he has revealed us to ourselves in revealing himself. And this recognition of purpose is, I believe, an essential part of the aesthetic judgment proper.

The perception of purposeful order and variety in an object gives us the feeling which we express by saying that it is beautiful, but when by means of sensations our emotions are aroused we demand purposeful order and variety in them also, and if this can only be brought about by the sacrifice of sensual beauty we willingly overlook its absence.

Thus, there is no excuse for a china pot being ugly, there is every reason why Rembrandt's and Degas' pictures should be, from the purely sensual point of view, supremely and magnificently ugly.

This, I think, will explain the apparent contradiction between two distinct uses of the word beauty, one for that which has sensuous charm, and one for the aesthetic approval of works of imaginative art where the objects presented to us are often of extreme ugliness. Beauty in the former sense belongs to works of art where only the perceptual aspect of the imaginative life is exercised, beauty in the second sense becomes as it were supersensual, and is concerned with the appropriateness and intensity of the emotions aroused. When these emotions are aroused in a way that satisfies fully the needs of the imaginative life we approve and delight in the sensations through which we enjoy that heightened experience because they possess purposeful order and variety in relation to those emotions.

Interpretive Questions

1. Why does Fry think there is every reason for some works of art to be ugly?

2. Does Fry think art can affect our actions?

3. How would Fry explain why some works of art gain immediate recognition and others gain recognition only after a long period of time?

4. Can an object created for use, such as a china pot, become a work of art?

5. Does the artist have a moral responsibility?

Writing Interpretive Questions

"An Essay in Aesthetics"

A reader made notes on a passage from "An Essay in Aesthetics" and then developed some of them into interpretive questions.

for whom?

response to art
differs from response
to actual life

imagination not
part of actual life?

all actions moral?—

art immoral?

Art, then, is an <u>expression and a</u>
<u>stimulus</u> of this imaginative life, which
is separated from actual life by the
absence of responsive action. Now this
responsive action implies in actual life
moral responsibility. In art (we) have no
such moral responsibility—it presents
a life freed from the binding necessities
of our actual existence. . .

*ambiguous:
viewer? artist? both?*

1. Does Fry think art cannot lead to action?

2. According to Fry, is art an expression and stimulus for the artist or for the viewer?

3. Are all actions either moral or immoral, according to Fry?

4. Does Fry think the artist has no moral responsibility?

5. Can art be immoral, according to Fry?

Using the example you have just read as a guide, make your own notes on the following passage, then turn those notes into interpretive questions.

> . . .Art, then, is, if I am right, the chief organ of the imaginative life; it is by art that it is stimulated and controlled within us, and, as we have seen, the imaginative life is distinguished by the greater clearness of its perception, and the greater purity and freedom of its emotion.

_____

_____

_____

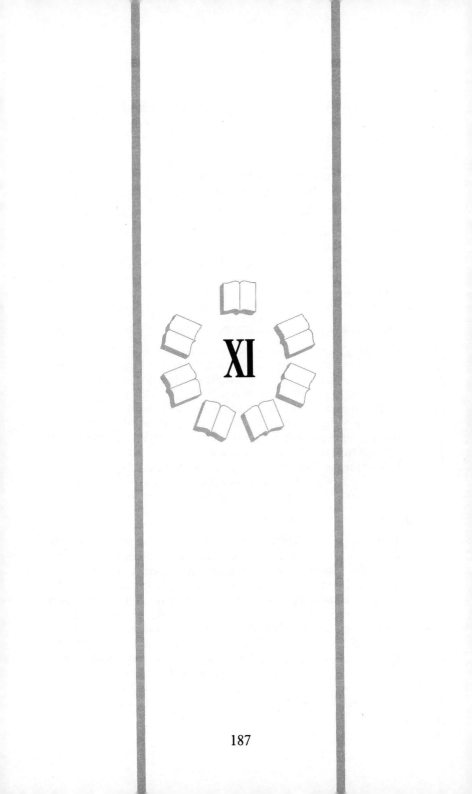

XI

By and About Joseph Conrad

(1857–1924)

Instead of appearing only "behind the draperies of fiction," Joseph Conrad also chose to stand "without disguise" in prefaces to some of his books. There he discusses his goal:

> My task . . . is, by the power of the written word to make you hear, to make you feel—it is, before all, to make you *see.* That—and no more, and it is everything. If I succeed, you shall find there according to your deserts: encouragement, consolation, fear, charm—all you demand—and, perhaps, also that glimpse of truth for which you have forgotten to ask.

On the appeal of art to emotion, not reason:

> [The artist] speaks to our capacity for delight and wonder, to the sense of mystery surrounding our lives; to our sense of pity, and beauty, and pain; to the latent feeling of fellowship with all creation—and to the subtle but invincible conviction of solidarity that knits together the loneliness of innumerable hearts. . . . It is only some such train of thought, or rather of feeling, that can . . . explain . . . the attempt . . . to present an unrestful episode in the obscure lives of a few individuals out of all the disregarded multitude of the bewildered, the simple, and the voiceless. For . . . there is not a place of splendor or a dark corner of the earth that does not deserve, if only a passing glance of wonder and pity.

On the power of language:

> You perceive the force of a word. He who wants to persuade should put his trust not in the right argument, but in the right word. The power of sound has always been greater than the power of sense. I don't say this by way of disparagement. It is better for mankind to be impressionable than reflective. Nothing humanly great—great, I mean, as affecting a whole mass of lives—has come from reflection. On the other hand, you cannot fail to see the power of mere words: such words as Glory, for instance, or Pity. I won't mention any more. They are not far to seek. Shouted with perseverance, with ardor, with conviction, these two by their sound alone have set whole nations in motion and upheaved the dry, hard ground on which rests our whole social fabric.

On his values:

Those who read me know my conviction that the world, the temporal world, rests on a few very simple ideas; so simple that they must be as old as the hills. It rests, notably, among others, on the idea of Fidelity. At a time when nothing which is not revolutionary in some way or other can expect to attract much attention, I have not been revolutionary in my writings. The revolutionary spirit is mighty convenient in this, that it frees one from all scruples as regards ideas. Its hard, absolute optimism is repulsive to my mind by the menace of fanaticism and intolerance it contains. No doubt, one should smile at these things; but, imperfect Aesthete, I am no better Philosopher. All claim to special righteousness awakens in me that scorn and anger from which a philosophical mind should be free.

An Outpost
of Progress

Joseph Conrad

I

There were two white men in charge of the trading station.
Kayerts, the chief, was short and fat; Carlier, the assistant, was
tall, with a large head and a very broad trunk perched upon
a long pair of thin legs. The third man on the staff was a Sierra
Leone nigger, who maintained that his name was Henry Price.
However, for some reason or other, the natives down the river
had given him the name of Makola, and it stuck to him through
all his wanderings about the country. He spoke English and
French with a warbling accent, wrote a beautiful hand, understood bookkeeping, and cherished in his innermost heart the
worship of evil spirits. His wife was a negress from Loanda,
very large and very noisy. Three children rolled about in sunshine before the door of his low, shed-like dwelling. Makola,
taciturn and impenetrable, despised the two white men. He
had charge of a small clay storehouse with a dried-grass roof,
and pretended to keep a correct account of beads, cotton cloth,

red kerchiefs, brass wire, and other trade goods it contained. Besides the storehouse and Makola's hut, there was only one large building in the cleared ground of the station. It was built neatly of reeds, with a verandah on all the four sides. There were three rooms in it. The one in the middle was the living room, and had two rough tables and a few stools in it. The other two were the bedrooms for the white men. Each had a bedstead and a mosquito net for all furniture. The plank floor was littered with the belongings of the white men; open half-empty boxes, torn wearing apparel, old boots; all the things dirty, and all the things broken, that accumulate mysteriously round untidy men. There was also another dwelling-place some distance away from the buildings. In it, under a tall cross much out of the perpendicular, slept the man who had seen the beginning of all this; who had planned and had watched the construction of this outpost of progress. He had been, at home, an unsuccessful painter who, weary of pursuing fame on an empty stomach, had gone out there through high protections. He had been the first chief of that station. Makola had watched the energetic artist die of fever in the just finished house with his usual kind of "I told you so" indifference. Then, for a time, he dwelt alone with his family, his account books, and the Evil Spirit that rules the lands under the equator. He got on very well with his god. Perhaps he had propitiated him by a promise of more white men to play with, by and by. At any rate the director of the Great Trading Company, coming up in a steamer that resembled an enormous sardine box with a flat-roofed shed erected on it, found the station in good order, and Makola as usual quietly diligent. The director had the cross put up over the first agent's grave, and appointed Kayerts to the post. Carlier was told off as second in charge. The director was a man ruthless and efficient, who at times, but very imperceptibly, indulged in grim humour. He made a speech to Kayerts and Carlier, pointing out to them the promising aspect of their station. The nearest trading-post was about three hundred miles away. It was an exceptional opportunity for them to distinguish themselves and to earn percentages on the trade. This appointment was a favour done to beginners. Kayerts was moved almost to tears by his director's kindness. He would, he said, by doing his best, try to justify the flattering confidence, &c., &c. Kayerts had been in the Administration of the Telegraphs, and knew how to express himself correctly. Carlier, an ex-noncommissioned officer of cavalry in an army guaranteed from harm by several European powers,* was less impressed. If there were commissions to get, so much the better; and, trailing a sulky glance over the river, the forests, the impenetrable bush that seemed to cut off the station from the rest of the world, he muttered between his teeth, "We shall see, very soon."

Next day, some bales of cotton goods and a few cases of provisions having been thrown on shore, the sardine-box steamer went off, not to return for another six months. On the deck the director touched his cap to the two agents, who stood on the bank waving their hats, and turning to an old servant of the Company on his passage to headquarters, said, "Look at those two imbeciles. They must be mad at home to send me such specimens. I told those fellows to plant a vegetable garden, build new storehouses and fences, and construct a landing stage. I bet nothing will be done! They won't know how to begin. I always thought the station on this river useless, and they just fit the station!"

"They will form themselves there," said the old stager with a quiet smile.

---

* *an army guaranteed from harm by several European powers.* The Belgian army.

"At any rate, I am rid of them for six months," retorted the director.

The two men watched the steamer round the bend, then, ascending arm in arm the slope of the bank, returned to the station. They had been in this vast and dark country only a very short time, and as yet always in the midst of other white men, under the eye and guidance of their superiors. And now, dull as they were to the subtle influences of surroundings, they felt themselves very much alone, when suddenly left unassisted to face the wilderness; a wilderness rendered more strange, more incomprehensible by the mysterious glimpses of the vigorous life it contained. They were two perfectly insignificant and incapable individuals, whose existence is only rendered possible through the high organization of civilized crowds. Few men realize that their life, the very essence of their character, their capabilities and their audacities, are only the expression of their belief in the safety of their surroundings. The courage, the composure, the confidence; the emotions and principles; every great and every insignificant thought belongs not to the individual but to the crowd: to the crowd that believes blindly in the irresistible force of its institutions and of its morals, in the power of its police and of its opinion. But the contact with pure unmitigated savagery, with primitive nature and primitive man, brings sudden and profound trouble into the heart. To the sentiment of being alone of one's kind, to the clear perception of the loneliness of one's thoughts, of one's sensations—to the negation of the habitual, which is safe, there is added the affirmation of the unusual, which is dangerous; a suggestion of things vague, uncontrollable, and repulsive, whose discomposing intrusion excites the imagination and tries the civilized nerves of the foolish and the wise alike.

Kayerts and Carlier walked arm in arm, drawing close to one another as children do in the dark; and they had the same, not altogether unpleasant, sense of danger which one half suspects to be imaginary. They chatted persistently in familiar tones. "Our station is prettily situated," said one. The other assented with enthusiasm, enlarging volubly on the beauties of the situation. Then they passed near the grave. "Poor devil!" said Kayerts. "He died of fever, didn't he?" muttered Carlier, stopping short. "Why," retorted Kayerts, with indignation, "I've been told that the fellow exposed himself recklessly to the sun. The climate here, everybody says, is not at all worse than at home, as long as you keep out of the sun. Do you hear that, Carlier? I am chief here, and my orders are that you should not expose yourself to the sun!" He assumed his superiority jocularly, but his meaning was serious. The idea that he would, perhaps, have to bury Carlier and remain alone, gave him an inward shiver. He felt suddenly that this Carlier was more precious to him here, in the centre of Africa, than a brother could be anywhere else. Carlier, entering into the spirit of the thing, made a military salute and answered in a brisk tone, "Your orders shall be attended to, chief!" Then he burst out laughing, slapped Kayerts on the back and shouted, "We shall let life run easily here! Just sit still and gather in the ivory those savages will bring. This country has its good points, after all!" They both laughed loudly while Carlier thought: "That poor Kayerts; he is so fat and unhealthy. It would be awful if I had to bury him here. He is a man I respect." ... Before they reached the verandah of their house they called one another "my dear fellow."

The first day they were very active, pottering about with hammers and nails and red calico, to put up curtains, make their house habitable and pretty; resolved to settle down comfortably to their new life. For them an impossible task. To grapple effectually with even purely material problems requires more serenity of mind and more lofty courage than people generally imagine. No two beings could have been more unfitted for such a struggle. Society, not from any tenderness, but because of its strange needs, had taken care of those two men, forbidding them all independent thought, all initiative, all departure from routine; and forbidding it under pain of death. They could only live on condition of being machines. And now, released from the fostering care of men with pens behind the ears, or of men with gold lace on the sleeves, they were like those lifelong prisoners who, liberated after many years, do not know what use to make of their freedom. They did not know what use to make of their faculties, being both, through want of practice, incapable of independent thought.

At the end of two months Kayerts often would say, "If it was not for my Melie, you wouldn't catch me here." Melie was his daughter. He had thrown up his post in the Administration of the Telegraphs, though he had been for seventeen years perfectly happy there, to earn a dowry for his girl. His wife was dead, and the child was being brought up by his sisters. He regretted* the streets, the pavements, the cafés, his friends of many years; all the things he used to see, day after day; all the thoughts suggested by familiar things—the thoughts effortless, monotonous, and soothing of a Government clerk; he regretted all the gossip, the small enmities, the mild venom, and the little jokes of Government offices. "If I had had a decent brother-in-law," Carlier would remark, "a fellow with a heart, I would not be here." He had left the army and had made himself so obnoxious to his family by his laziness and impudence, that an exasperated brother-in-law had made superhuman efforts to procure him an appointment in the Company as a second-class agent. Having not a penny in the world he

---

* *regretted.* Missed.

was compelled to accept this means of livelihood as soon as it became quite clear to him that there was nothing more to squeeze out of his relations. He, like Kayerts, regretted his old life. He regretted the clink of sabre and spurs on a fine afternoon, the barrack room witticisms, the girls of garrison towns; but, besides, he had also a sense of grievance. He was evidently a much ill-used man. This made him moody, at times. But the two men got on well together in the fellowship of their stupidity and laziness. Together they did nothing, absolutely nothing, and enjoyed the sense of the idleness for which they were paid. And in time they came to feel something resembling affection for one another.

They lived like blind men in a large room, aware only of what came in contact with them (and of that only imperfectly), but unable to see the general aspect of things. The river, the forest, all the great land throbbing with life, were like a great emptiness. Even the brilliant sunshine disclosed nothing intelligible. Things appeared and disappeared before their eyes in an unconnected and aimless kind of way. The river seemed to come from nowhere and flow nowhither. It flowed through a void. Out of that void, at times, came canoes, and men with spears in their hands would suddenly crowd the yard of the station. They were naked, glossy black, ornamented with snowy shells and glistening brass wire, perfect of limb. They made an uncouth babbling noise when they spoke, moved in a stately manner, and sent quick, wild glances out of their startled, never-resting eyes. Those warriors would squat in long rows, four or more deep, before the verandah, while their chiefs bargained for hours with Makola over an elephant tusk. Kayerts sat on his chair and looked down on the proceedings, understanding nothing. He stared at them with his round blue eyes, called out to Carlier, "Here, look! look at that fellow there— and that other one, to the left. Did you ever see such a face? Oh, the funny brute!"

Carlier, smoking native tobacco in a short wooden pipe, would swagger up twirling his moustaches, and surveying the warriors with haughty indulgence, would say:

"Fine animals. Brought any bone? Yes? It's not any too soon. Look at the muscles of that fellow—third from the end. I wouldn't care to get a punch on the nose from him. Fine arms, but legs no good below the knee. Couldn't make cavalry men of them." And after glancing down complacently at his own shanks, he always concluded: "Pah! Don't they stink! You, Makola! Take that herd over to the fetish" (the storehouse was in every station called the fetish, perhaps because of the spirit of civilization it contained) "and give them up some of the rubbish you keep there. I'd rather see it full of bone than full of rags."

Kayerts approved.

"Yes, yes! Go and finish that palaver over there, Mr. Makola. I will come round when you are ready, to weigh the tusk. We must be careful." Then turning to his companion: "This is the tribe that lives down the river; they are rather aromatic. I remember, they had been once before here. D'ye hear that row? What a fellow has got to put up with in this dog of a country! My head is split."

Such profitable visits were rare. For days the two pioneers of trade and progress would look on their empty courtyard in the vibrating brilliance of vertical sunshine. Below the high bank, the silent river flowed on glittering and steady. On the sands in the middle of the stream, hippos and alligators sunned themselves side by side. And stretching away in all directions, surrounding the insignificant cleared spot of the trading post, immense forests, hiding fateful complications of fantastic life, lay in the eloquent silence of mute greatness. The two men understood nothing, cared for nothing but for the passage of days that separated them from the steamer's return. Their predecessor had left some torn books. They took up these wrecks of novels, and, as they had never read anything of the kind before, they were surprised and amused. Then during long days there were interminable and silly discussions about plots and personages. In the centre of Africa they made acquaintance of Richelieu and of d'Artagnan, of Hawk's Eye and of Father Goriot, and of many other people.* All these imaginary personages became subjects for gossip as if they had been living friends. They discounted their virtues, suspected their motives, decried their successes; were scandalized at their duplicity or were doubtful about their courage. The accounts of crimes filled them with indignation, while tender or pathetic passages moved them deeply. Carlier cleared his throat and said in a soldierly voice, "What nonsense!" Kayerts, his round eyes suffused with tears, his fat cheeks quivering, rubbed his bald head, and declared, "This is a splendid book. I had no idea there were such clever fellows in the world." They also found some old copies of a home paper. That print discussed what it was pleased to call "Our Colonial Expansion" in high-flown language. It spoke much of the rights and duties of civilization, of the sacredness of the civilizing work, and extolled the merits of those who went about bringing light and faith and commerce to the dark places of the earth. Carlier and Kayerts read, wondered, and began to think better of themselves. Carlier said one evening, waving his hand about, "In a hundred years, there will be perhaps a town here. Quays, and warehouses, and barracks, and—and—billiard-rooms. Civilization, my boy, and virtue—and all. And then, chaps will read that two good fel-

---

* Richelieu and d'Artagnan are characters in Alexander Dumas' *The Three Musketeers*, Hawk's Eye (usually spelled Hawkeye) is in *The Last of the Mohicans*, and Father Goriot is in the novel *Father Goriot* by Honoré de Balzac.

lows, Kayerts and Carlier, were the first civilized men to live in this very spot!" Kayerts nodded, "Yes, it is a consolation to think of that." They seemed to forget their dead predecessor; but, early one day, Carlier went out and replanted the cross firmly. "It used to make me squint whenever I walked that way," he explained to Kayerts over the morning coffee. "It made me squint, leaning over so much. So I just planted it upright. And solid, I promise you! I suspended myself with both hands to the cross-piece. Not a move. Oh, I did that properly."

At times Gobila came to see them. Gobila was the chief of the neighbouring villages. He was a gray-headed savage, thin and black, with a white cloth round his loins and a mangy panther skin hanging over his back. He came up with long strides of his skeleton legs, swinging a staff as tall as himself, and, entering the common room of the station, would squat on his heels to the left of the door. There he sat, watching Kayerts, and now and then making a speech which the other did not understand. Kayerts, without interrupting his occupation, would from time to time say in a friendly manner: "How goes it, you old image?" and they would smile at one another. The two whites had a liking for that old and incomprehensible creature, and called him Father Gobila. Gobila's manner was paternal, and he seemed really to love all white men. They all appeared to him very young, indistinguishably alike (except for stature), and he knew that they were all brothers, and also immortal. The death of the artist, who was the first white man whom he knew intimately, did not disturb this belief, because he was firmly convinced that the white stranger had pretended to die and got himself buried for some mysterious purpose of his own, into which it was useless to inquire. Perhaps it was his way of going home to his own country? At any rate, these were his brothers, and he transferred his absurd affection to them.

They returned it in a way. Carlier slapped him on the back, and recklessly struck off matches for his amusement. Kayerts was always ready to let him have a sniff at the ammonia bottle. In short, they behaved just like that other white creature that had hidden itself in a hole in the ground. Gobila considered them attentively. Perhaps they were the same being with the other—or one of them was. He couldn't decide—clear up that mystery; but he remained always very friendly. In consequence of that friendship the women of Gobila's village walked in single file through the reedy grass, bringing every morning to the station, fowls, and sweet potatoes, and palm wine, and sometimes a goat. The Company never provisions the stations fully, and the agents required those local supplies to live. They had them through the goodwill of Gobila, and lived well. Now and then one of them had a bout of fever, and the other nursed him with gentle devotion. They did not think much of it. It left them weaker, and their appearance changed for the worse. Carlier was hollow-eyed and irritable. Kayerts showed a drawn, flabby face above the rotundity of his stomach, which gave him a weird aspect. But being constantly together, they did not notice the change that took place gradually in their appearance, and also in their dispositions.

Five months passed in that way.

Then, one morning, as Kayerts and Carlier, lounging in their chairs under the verandah, talked about the approaching visit of the steamer, a knot of armed men came out of the forest and advanced towards the station. They were strangers to that part of the country. They were tall, slight, draped classically from neck to heel in blue fringed cloths, and carried percussion muskets over their bare right shoulders. Makola showed signs of excitement, and ran out of the storehouse (where he spent all his days) to meet these visitors. They came into the courtyard and looked about them with steady, scornful glances.

Their leader, a powerful and determined-looking negro with bloodshot eyes, stood in front of the verandah and made a long speech. He gesticulated much, and ceased very suddenly.

There was something in his intonation, in the sounds of the long sentences he used, that startled the two whites. It was like a reminiscence of something not exactly familiar, and yet resembling the speech of civilized men. It sounded like one of those impossible languages which sometimes we hear in our dreams.

"What lingo is that?" said the amazed Carlier. "In the first moment I fancied the fellow was going to speak French. Anyway, it is a different kind of gibberish to what we ever heard."

"Yes," replied Kayerts. "Hey, Makola, what does he say? Where do they come from? Who are they?"

But Makola, who seemed to be standing on hot bricks, answered hurriedly, "I don't know. They come from very far. Perhaps Mrs. Price will understand. They are perhaps bad men."

The leader, after waiting for a while, said something sharply to Makola, who shook his head. Then the man, after looking round, noticed Makola's hut and walked over there. The next moment Mrs. Makola was heard speaking with great volubility. The other strangers—they were six in all—strolled about with an air of ease, put their heads through the door of the storeroom, congregated round the grave, pointed understandingly at the cross, and generally made themselves at home.

"I don't like those chaps—and, I say, Kayerts, they must be from the coast; they've got firearms," observed the sagacious Carlier.

Kayerts also did not like those chaps. They both, for the first time, became aware that they lived in conditions where the unusual may be dangerous, and that there was no power on earth outside of themselves to stand between them and the

unusual. They became uneasy, went in and loaded their re-
volvers. Kayerts said, "We must order Makola to tell them to
go away before dark."

The strangers left in the afternoon, after eating a meal
prepared for them by Mrs. Makola. The immense woman was
excited, and talked much with the visitors. She rattled away
shrilly, pointing here and there at the forests and at the river.
Makola sat apart and watched. At times he got up and whispered to his wife. He accompanied the strangers across the
ravine at the back of the station ground, and returned slowly
looking very thoughtful. When questioned by the white men
he was very strange, seemed not to understand, seemed to have
forgotten French—seemed to have forgotten how to speak
altogether. Kayerts and Carlier agreed that the nigger had had
too much palm wine.

There was some talk about keeping a watch in turn, but in
the evening everything seemed so quiet and peaceful that they
retired as usual. All night they were disturbed by a lot of
drumming in the villages. A deep, rapid roll near by would be
followed by another far off—then all ceased. Soon short ap-
peals would rattle out here and there, then all mingle together,
increase, become vigorous and sustained, would spread out
over the forest, roll through the night, unbroken and ceaseless,
near and far, as if the whole land had been one immense drum
booming out steadily an appeal to heaven. And through the
deep and tremendous noise sudden yells that resembled snatches
of songs from a madhouse darted shrill and high in discordant
jets of sound which seemed to rush far above the earth and
drive all peace from under the stars.

Carlier and Kayerts slept badly. They both thought they had
heard shots fired during the night—but they could not agree
as to the direction. In the morning Makola was gone some-
where. He returned about noon with one of yesterday's stran-

gers, and eluded all Kayerts' attempts to close with him: had become deaf apparently. Kayerts wondered. Carlier, who had been fishing off the bank, came back and remarked while he showed his catch, "The niggers seem to be in a deuce of a stir; I wonder what's up. I saw about fifteen canoes cross the river during the two hours I was there fishing." Kayerts, worried, said, "Isn't this Makola very queer today?" Carlier advised, "Keep all our men together in case of some trouble."

II

There were ten station men who had been left by the Director. Those fellows, having engaged themselves to the Company for six months (without having any idea of a month in particular and only a very faint notion of time in general), had been serving the cause of progress for upwards of two years. Belonging to a tribe from a very distant part of the land of darkness and sorrow, they did not run away, naturally supposing that as wandering strangers they would be killed by the inhabitants of the country; in which they were right. They lived in straw huts on the slope of a ravine overgrown with reedy grass, just behind the station buildings. They were not happy, regretting the festive incantations, the sorceries, the human sacrifices of their own land; where they also had parents, brothers, sisters, admired chiefs, respected magicians, loved friends, and other ties supposed generally to be human. Besides, the rice rations served out by the Company did not agree with them, being a food unknown to their land, and to which they could not get used. Consequently they were unhealthy and miserable. Had they been of any other tribe they would have made up their minds to die—for nothing is easier to certain savages than suicide—and so have escaped from the puzzling difficulties of existence. But belonging, as they did, to a warlike tribe with filed teeth, they had more grit, and went on stupidly living through disease and sorrow. They did very little work, and had lost their splendid physique. Carlier and Kayerts doctored them assiduously without being able to bring them back into condition again. They were mustered every morning and told off to different tasks—grass cutting, fence building, tree felling, &c., &c., which no power on earth could induce them to execute efficiently. The two whites had practically very little control over them.

In the afternoon Makola came over to the big house and found Kayerts watching three heavy columns of smoke rising above the forests. "What is that?" asked Kayerts. "Some villages burn," answered Makola, who seemed to have regained his wits. Then he said abruptly: "We have got very little ivory; bad six months' trading. Do you like get a little more ivory?"

"Yes," said Kayerts, eagerly. He thought of percentages which were low.

"Those men who came yesterday are traders from Loanda who have got more ivory than they can carry home. Shall I buy? I know their camp."

"Certainly," said Kayerts. "What are those traders?"

"Bad fellows," said Makola, indifferently. "They fight with people, and catch women and children. They are bad men, and got guns. There is a great disturbance in the country. Do you want ivory?"

"Yes," said Kayerts. Makola said nothing for a while. Then: "Those workmen of ours are no good at all," he muttered, looking round. "Station in very bad order, sir. Director will growl. Better get a fine lot of ivory, then he say nothing."

"I can't help it; the men won't work," said Kayerts. "When will you get that ivory?"

"Very soon," said Makola. "Perhaps tonight. You leave it to me, and keep indoors, sir. I think you had better give some palm wine to our men to make a dance this evening. Enjoy themselves. Work better tomorrow. There's plenty palm wine—gone a little sour."

Kayerts said "yes," and Makola, with his own hands carried big calabashes to the door of his hut. They stood there till the evening, and Mrs. Makola looked into every one. The men got them at sunset. When Kayerts and Carlier retired, a big bonfire was flaring before the men's huts. They could hear their shouts and drumming. Some men from Gobila's village had joined the station hands, and the entertainment was a great success.

In the middle of the night, Carlier, waking suddenly, heard a man shout loudly; then a shot was fired. Only one. Carlier ran out and met Kayerts on the verandah. They were both startled. As they went across the yard to call Makola, they saw shadows moving in the night. One of them cried, "Don't shoot! It's me, Price." Then Makola appeared close to them. "Go back, go back, please," he urged, "you spoil all." "There are strange men about," said Carlier. "Never mind; I know," said Makola. Then he whispered, "All right. Bring ivory. Say nothing! I know my business." The two white men reluctantly went back to the house, but did not sleep. They heard footsteps, whispers, some groans. It seemed as if a lot of men came in, dumped heavy things on the ground, squabbled a long time, then went away. They lay on their hard beds and thought: "This Makola is invaluable." In the morning Carlier came out, very sleepy, and pulled at the cord of the big bell. The station hands mustered every morning to the sound of the bell. That morning nobody came. Kayerts turned out also, yawning. Across the yard they saw Makola come out of his hut, a tin basin of soapy water in his hand. Makola, a civilized nigger, was very neat in his person. He threw the soapsuds skilfully over a wretched little yellow cur he had, then turning his face to the agent's house, he shouted from the distance, "All the men gone last night!"

They heard him plainly, but in their surprise they both yelled out together: "What!" Then they stared at one another. "We are in a proper fix now," growled Carlier. "It's incredible!" muttered Kayerts. "I will go to the huts and see," said Carlier, striding off. Makola coming up found Kayerts standing alone.

"I can hardly believe it," said Kayerts, tearfully. "We took care of them as if they had been our children."

"They went with the coast people," said Makola after a moment of hesitation.

"What do I care with whom they went—the ungrateful brutes!" exclaimed the other. Then with sudden suspicion, and looking hard at Makola, he added: "What do you know about it?"

Makola moved his shoulders, looking down on the ground. "What do I know? I think only. Will you come and look at the ivory I've got there? It is a fine lot. You never saw such."

He moved towards the store. Kayerts followed him mechanically, thinking about the incredible desertion of the men. On the ground before the door of the fetish lay six splendid tusks.

"What did you give for it?" asked Kayerts, after surveying the lot with satisfaction.

"No regular trade," said Makola. "They brought the ivory and gave it to me. I told them to take what they most wanted in the station. It is a beautiful lot. No station can show such tusks. Those traders wanted carriers badly, and our men were no good here. No trade, no entry in books; all correct."

Kayerts nearly burst with indignation. "Why!" he shouted, "I believe you have sold our men for these tusks!" Makola stood impassive and silent. "I—I—will—I," stuttered Kayerts. "You fiend!" he yelled out.

"I did the best for you and the Company," said Makola, imperturbably. "Why you shout so much? Look at this tusk."

"I dismiss you! I will report you—I won't look at the tusk. I forbid you to touch them. I order you to throw them into the river. You—you!"

"You very red, Mr. Kayerts. If you are so irritable in the sun, you will get fever and die—like the first chief!" pronounced Makola impressively.

They stood still, contemplating one another with intense eyes, as if they had been looking with effort across immense distances. Kayerts shivered. Makola had meant no more than he said, but his words seemed to Kayerts full of ominous menace! He turned sharply and went away to the house. Makola retired into the bosom of his family; and the tusks, left lying before the store, looked very large and valuable in the sunshine.

Carlier came back on the verandah. "They're all gone, hey?" asked Kayerts from the far end of the common room in a muffled voice. "You did not find anybody?"

"Oh, yes," said Carlier, "I found one of Gobila's people lying dead before the huts—shot through the body. We heard that shot last night."

Kayerts came out quickly. He found his companion staring grimly over the yard at the tusks, away by the store. They both sat in silence for a while. Then Kayerts related his conversation with Makola. Carlier said nothing. At the midday meal they ate very little. They hardly exchanged a word that day. A great silence seemed to lie heavily over the station and press on their lips. Makola did not open the store; he spent the day playing with his children. He lay full-length on a mat outside his door, and the youngsters sat on his chest and clambered all over him. It was a touching picture. Mrs. Makola was busy cooking all day as usual. The white men made a somewhat better meal in the evening. Afterwards, Carlier smoking his pipe strolled over to the store; he stood for a long time over the tusks, touched one or two with his foot, even tried to lift the largest one by its small end. He came back to his chief, who had not stirred from the verandah, threw himself in the chair and said:

"I can see it! They were pounced upon while they slept heavily after drinking all that palm wine you've allowed Makola to give them. A put-up job! See? The worst is, some of Gobila's people were there, and got carried off too, no doubt. The least drunk woke up, and got shot for his sobriety. This is a funny country. What will you do now?"

"We can't touch it, of course," said Kayerts.

"Of course not," assented Carlier.

"Slavery is an awful thing," stammered out Kayerts in an unsteady voice.

"Frightful—the sufferings," grunted Carlier with conviction.

They believed their words. Everybody shows a respectful deference to certain sounds that he and his fellows can make. But about feelings people really know nothing. We talk with indignation or enthusiasm; we talk about oppression, cruelty, crime, devotion, self-sacrifice, virtue, and we know nothing real beyond the words. Nobody knows what suffering or sacrifice mean—except, perhaps, the victims of the mysterious purpose of these illusions.

Next morning they saw Makola very busy setting up in the yard the big scales used for weighing ivory. By and by Carlier said: "What's that filthy scoundrel up to?" and lounged out into the yard. Kayerts followed. They stood watching. Makola took no notice. When the balance was swung true, he tried to lift a tusk into the scale. It was too heavy. He looked up helplessly without a word, and for a minute they stood round that balance as mute and still as three statues. Suddenly Carlier said: "Catch hold of the other end, Makola—you beast!" and together they swung the tusk up. Kayerts trembled in every limb. He muttered, "I say! O! I say!" and putting his hand in his pocket found there a dirty bit of paper and the stump of a pencil. He turned his back on the others, as if about to do something tricky, and noted stealthily the weights which Carlier shouted out to him with unnecessary loudness. When all was over Makola whispered to himself: "The sun's very strong here for the tusks." Carlier said to Kayerts in a careless tone: "I say, chief, I might just as well give him a lift with this lot into the store."

As they were going back to the house Kayerts observed with a sigh: "It had to be done." And Carlier said: "It's deplorable, but, the men being Company's men the ivory is Company's ivory. We must look after it." "I will report to the Director, of course," said Kayerts. "Of course; let him decide," approved Carlier.

At midday they made a hearty meal. Kayerts sighed from time to time. Whenever they mentioned Makola's name they always added to it an opprobrious epithet. It eased their conscience. Makola gave himself a half-holiday, and bathed his children in the river. No one from Gobila's villages came near the station that day. No one came the next day, and the next, nor for a whole week. Gobila's people might have been dead and buried for any sign of life they gave. But they were only mourning for those they had lost by the witchcraft of white men, who had brought wicked people into their country. The wicked people were gone, but fear remained. Fear always remains. A man may destroy everything within himself, love and hate and belief, and even doubt; but as long as he clings to life he cannot destroy fear: the fear, subtle, indestructible, and terrible, that pervades his being; that tinges his thoughts; that lurks in his heart; that watches on his lips the struggle of his last breath. In his fear, the mild old Gobila offered extra human sacrifices to all the Evil Spirits that had taken possession of his white friends. His heart was heavy. Some warriors spoke about burning and killing, but the cautious old savage dissuaded them. Who could foresee the woe those mysterious creatures, if irritated, might bring? They should be left alone. Perhaps in time they would disappear into the earth as the first one had disappeared. His people must keep away from them, and hope for the best.

Kayerts and Carlier did not disappear, but remained above on this earth, that, somehow, they fancied had become bigger and very empty. It was not the absolute and dumb solitude of the post that impressed them so much as an inarticulate feeling that something from within them was gone, something that worked for their safety, and had kept the wilderness from interfering with their hearts. The images of home; the memory of people like them, of men that thought and felt as they used to think and feel, receded into distances made indistinct by the glare of unclouded sunshine. And out of the great silence of the surrounding wilderness, its very hopelessness and savagery seemed to approach them nearer, to draw them gently, to look upon them, to envelop them with a solicitude irresistible, familiar, and disgusting.

Days lengthened into weeks, then into months. Gobila's people drummed and yelled to every new moon, as of yore, but kept away from the station. Makola and Carlier tried once in a canoe to open communications, but were received with a shower of arrows, and had to fly back to the station for dear life. That attempt set the country up and down the river into an uproar that could be very distinctly heard for days. The steamer was late. At first they spoke of delay jauntily, then anxiously, then gloomily. The matter was becoming serious. Stores were running short. Carlier cast his lines off the bank, but the river was low, and the fish kept out in the stream. They dared not stroll far away from the station to shoot. Moreover, there was no game in the impenetrable forest. Once Carlier shot a hippo in the river. They had no boat to secure it, and it sank. When it floated up it drifted away, and Gobila's people secured the carcass. It was the occasion for a national holiday, but Carlier had a fit of rage over it and talked about the necessity of exterminating all the niggers before the country could be made habitable. Kayerts mooned about silently; spent hours looking at the portrait of his Melie. It represented a little girl with long bleached tresses and a rather sour face. His legs were much swollen, and he could hardly walk. Carlier, undermined by fever, could not swagger any more, but kept tottering about, still with a devil-may-care air, as became a man who remembered his crack regiment. He had become hoarse, sarcastic, and inclined to say unpleasant things. He called it "being frank with you." They had long ago reckoned their percentages on trade, including in them that last deal of "this infamous Makola." They had also concluded not to say anything about it. Kayerts hesitated at first—was afraid of the Director.

"He has seen worse things done on the quiet," maintained Carlier, with a hoarse laugh. "Trust him! He won't thank you if you blab. He is no better than you or me. Who will talk if we hold our tongues? There is nobody here."

That was the root of the trouble! There was nobody there; and being left there alone with their weakness, they became daily more like a pair of accomplices than like a couple of devoted friends. They had heard nothing from home for eight months. Every evening they said, "Tomorrow we shall see the steamer." But one of the Company's steamers had been wrecked, and the Director was busy with the other, relieving very distant and important stations on the main river. He thought that the useless station, and the useless men, could wait. Meantime Kayerts and Carlier lived on rice boiled without salt, and cursed the Company, all Africa, and the day they were born. One must have lived on such diet to discover what ghastly trouble the necessity of swallowing one's food may become. There was literally nothing else in the station but rice and coffee; they drank the coffee without sugar. The last fifteen lumps Kayerts had solemnly locked away in his box, together with a half-bottle of cognac, "in case of sickness," he explained. Carlier approved. "When one is sick," he said, "any little extra like that is cheering."

They waited. Rank grass began to sprout over the courtyard. The bell never rang now. Days passed, silent, exasperating, and slow. When the two men spoke, they snarled; and their silences were bitter, as if tinged by the bitterness of their thoughts.

One day after a lunch of boiled rice, Carlier put down his cup untasted, and said: "Hang it all! Let's have a decent cup of coffee for once. Bring out that sugar, Kayerts!"

"For the sick," muttered Kayerts, without looking up.

"For the sick," mocked Carlier. "Bosh! . . . Well! I am sick."

"You are no more sick that I am, and I go without," said Kayerts in a peaceful tone.

"Come! out with that sugar, you stingy old slave-dealer."

Kayerts looked up quickly. Carlier was smiling with marked insolence. And suddenly it seemed to Kayerts that he had never seen that man before. Who was he? He knew nothing about him. What was he capable of? There was a surprising flash of violent emotion within him, as if in the presence of something undreamt-of, dangerous, and final. But he managed to pronounce with composure:

"That joke is in very bad taste. Don't repeat it."

"Joke!" said Carlier, hitching himself forward on his seat. "I am hungry—I am sick—I don't joke! I hate hypocrites. You are a hypocrite. You are a slave-dealer. I am a slave-dealer.

There's nothing but slave-dealers in this cursed country. I mean to have sugar in my coffee today, anyhow!"

"I forbid you to speak to me in that way," said Kayerts with a fair show of resolution.

"You!—What?" shouted Carlier, jumping up.

Kayerts stood up also. "I am your chief," he began, trying to master the shakiness of his voice.

"What?" yelled the other. "Who's chief? There's no chief here. There's nothing here: there's nothing but you and I. Fetch the sugar—you pot-bellied ass."

"Hold your tongue. Go out of this room," screamed Kayerts. "I dismiss you—you scoundrel!"

Carlier swung a stool. All at once he looked dangerously in earnest. "You flabby, good-for-nothing civilian—take that!" he howled.

Kayerts dropped under the table, and the stool struck the grass inner wall of the room. Then, as Carlier was trying to upset the table, Kayerts in desperation made a blind rush, head low, like a cornered pig would do, and overturning his friend, bolted along the verandah, and into his room. He locked the door, snatched his revolver, and stood panting. In less than a minute Carlier was kicking at the door furiously, howling, "If you don't bring out that sugar, I will shoot you at sight, like a dog. Now then—one—two—three. You won't? I will show you who's the master."

Kayerts thought the door would fall in, and scrambled through the square hole that served for a window in his room. There was then the whole breadth of the house between them. But the other was apparently not strong enough to break in the door, and Kayerts heard him running round. Then he also began to run laboriously on his swollen legs. He ran as quickly as he could, grasping the revolver, and unable yet to understand what was happening to him. He saw in succession Makola's house, the store, the river, the ravine, and the low bushes; and he saw all those things again as he ran for the second time round the house. Then again they flashed past him. That morning he could not have walked a yard without a groan.

And now he ran. He ran fast enough to keep out of sight of the other man.

Then as, weak and desperate, he thought, "Before I finish the next round I shall die," he heard the other man stumble heavily, then stop. He stopped also. He had the back and Carlier the front of the house, as before. He heard him drop into a chair cursing, and suddenly his own legs gave way, and he slid down into a sitting posture with his back to the wall. His mouth was as dry as a cinder, and his face was wet with perspiration—and tears. What was it all about? He thought it must be a horrible illusion; he thought he was dreaming; he thought he was going mad! After a while he collected his senses. What did they quarrel about? That sugar! How absurd! He would give it to him—didn't want it himself. And he began scrambling to his feet with a sudden feeling of security. But before he had fairly stood upright, a common-sense reflection occurred to him and drove him back into despair. He thought: "If I give way now to that brute of a soldier, he will begin this horror again tomorrow—and the day after—every day—raise other pretensions, trample on me, torture me, make me his slave—and I will be lost! Lost! The steamer may not come for days—may never come." He shook so that he had to sit down on the floor again. He shivered forlornly. He felt he could not, would not move any more. He was completely distracted by the sudden perception that the position was without issue— that death and life had in a moment become equally difficult and terrible.

All at once he heard the other push his chair back; and he leaped to his feet with extreme facility. He listened and got confused. Must run again! Right or left? He heard footsteps. He darted to the left, grasping his revolver, and at the very same instant, as it seemed to him, they came into violent collision. Both shouted with surprise. A loud explosion took place between them; a roar of red fire, thick smoke; and Kayerts, deafened and blinded, rushed back thinking: "I am hit—it's all over." He expected the other to come round—to gloat over his agony. He caught hold of an upright of the roof: "All over!" Then he heard a crashing fall on the other side of the house, as if somebody had tumbled headlong over a chair—then silence. Nothing more happened. He did not die. Only his shoulder felt as if it had been badly wrenched, and he had lost his revolver. He was disarmed and helpless! He waited for his fate. The other man made no sound. It was a stratagem. He was stalking him now! Along what side? Perhaps he was taking aim this very minute!

After a few moments of an agony frightful and absurd, he decided to go and meet his doom. He was prepared for every surrender. He turned the corner, steadying himself with one hand on the wall; made a few paces, and nearly swooned. He had seen on the floor, protruding past the other corner, a pair of turned-up feet. A pair of white naked feet in red slippers. He felt deadly sick, and stood for a time in profound darkness. Then Makola appeared before him, saying quietly: "Come along, Mr. Kayerts. He is dead." He burst into tears of gratitude; a loud, sobbing fit of crying. After a time he found himself sitting in a chair and looking at Carlier, who lay stretched on his back. Makola was kneeling over the body.

"Is this your revolver?" asked Makola, getting up.

"Yes," said Kayerts; then he added very quickly, "He ran after me to shoot me—you saw!"

"Yes, I saw," said Makola. "There is only one revolver; where's his?"

"Don't know," whispered Kayerts in a voice that had become suddenly very faint.

"I will go and look for it," said the other, gently. He made the round along the verandah, while Kayerts sat still and looked at the corpse. Makola came back empty-handed, stood in deep thought, then stepped quietly into the dead man's room, and came out directly with a revolver, which he held up before Kayerts. Kayerts shut his eyes. Everything was going round. He found life more terrible and difficult than death. He had shot an unarmed man.

After meditating for a while, Makola said softly, pointing at the dead man who lay there with his right eye blown out:

"He died of fever." Kayerts looked at him with a stony stare. "Yes," repeated Makola, thoughtfully, stepping over the corpse, "I think he died of fever. Bury him tomorrow."

And he went away slowly to his expectant wife, leaving the two white men alone on the verandah.

Night came, and Kayerts sat unmoving on his chair. He sat quiet as if he had taken a dose of opium. The violence of the emotions he had passed through produced a feeling of exhausted serenity. He had plumbed in one short afternoon the depths of horror and despair, and now found repose in the conviction that life had no more secrets for him: neither had death! He sat by the corpse thinking; thinking very actively, thinking very new thoughts. He seemed to have broken loose from himself altogether. His old thoughts, convictions, likes and dislikes, things he respected and things he abhorred, appeared in their true light at last! Appeared contemptible and childish, false and ridiculous. He revelled in his new wisdom while he sat by the man he had killed. He argued with himself about all things under heaven with that kind of wrong-headed lucidity which may be observed in some lunatics. Incidentally he reflected that the fellow dead there had been a noxious beast anyway; that men died every day in thousands; perhaps in hundreds of thousands—who could tell?—and that in the number, that one death could not possibly make any difference; couldn't have any importance, at least to a thinking creature. He, Kayerts, was a thinking creature. He had been all his life, till that moment, a believer in a lot of nonsense like the rest of mankind—who are fools; but now he thought! He knew! He was at peace; he was familiar with the highest wisdom! Then he tried to imagine himself dead, and Carlier sitting in his chair watching him; and his attempt met with such unexpected success, that in a very few moments he became not at all sure who was dead and who was alive. This extraordinary achievement of his fancy startled him, however, and by a clever and timely effort of mind he saved himself just in time from becoming Carlier. His heart thumped, and he felt hot all over at the thought of that danger. Carlier! What a beastly thing! To compose his now disturbed nerves—and no wonder!—he tried to whistle a little. Then, suddenly, he fell asleep, or thought he had slept; but at any rate there was a fog, and somebody had whistled in the fog.

He stood up. The day had come, and a heavy mist had descended upon the land: the mist penetrating, enveloping, and silent; the morning mist of tropical lands; the mist that clings and kills; the mist white and deadly, immaculate and poisonous. He stood up, saw the body, and threw his arms above his head with a cry like that of a man who, waking from a trance, finds himself immured forever in a tomb. *"Help! . . . My God!"*

A shriek inhuman, vibrating and sudden, pierced like a sharp dart the white shroud of that land of sorrow. Three short, impatient screeches followed, and then, for a time, the fog-wreaths rolled on, undisturbed, through a formidable silence. Then many more shrieks, rapid and piercing, like the yells of some exasperated and ruthless creature, rent the air. Progress was calling to Kayerts from the river. Progress and civilization and all the virtues. Society was calling to its accomplished child to come, to be taken care of, to be instructed, to be judged, to be condemned; it called him to return to that rubbish heap from which he had wandered away, so that justice could be done.

Kayerts heard and understood. He stumbled out of the verandah, leaving the other man quite alone for the first time since they had been thrown there together. He groped his way through the fog, calling in his ignorance upon the invisible heaven to undo its work. Makola flitted by in the mist, shouting as he ran:

"Steamer! Steamer! They can't see. They whistle for the station. I go ring the bell. Go down to the landing, sir. I ring."

He disappeared. Kayerts stood still. He looked upwards; the fog rolled low over his head. He looked round like a man who has lost his way; and he saw a dark smudge, a cross-shaped stain, upon the shifting purity of the mist. As he began to stumble towards it, the station bell rang in a tumultuous peal its answer to the impatient clamour of the steamer.

The Managing Director of the Great Civilizing Company (since we know that civilization follows trade) landed first, and incontinently lost sight of the steamer. The fog down by the river was exceedingly dense; above, at the station, the bell rang unceasing and brazen.

The Director shouted loudly to the steamer:

"There is nobody down to meet us; there may be something wrong, though they are ringing. You had better come, too!"

And he began to toil up the steep bank. The captain and the engine driver of the boat followed behind. As they scrambled up the fog thinned, and they could see their Director a good way ahead. Suddenly they saw him start forward, calling to them over his shoulder: "Run! Run to the house! I've found one of them. Run, look for the other!"

He had found one of them! And even he, the man of varied and startling experience, was somewhat discomposed by the manner of this finding. He stood and fumbled in his pockets (for a knife) while he faced Kayerts, who was hanging by a leather strap from the cross. He had evidently climbed the grave, which was high and narrow, and after tying the end of the strap to the arm, had swung himself off. His toes were only a couple of inches above the ground; his arms hung stiffly down; he seemed to be standing rigidly at attention, but with one purple cheek playfully posed on the shoulder. And, irreverently, he was putting out a swollen tongue at his Managing Director.

Interpretive Questions

1. Could Makola have refused to give the ten station men to the armed stranger?

2. What brings about the disintegration of Kayerts and Carlier?

3. Why does Kayerts hang himself?

4. What does Conrad mean by "civilization"?

5. If Conrad is criticizing civilization, why does he present the plundered natives as less than human?

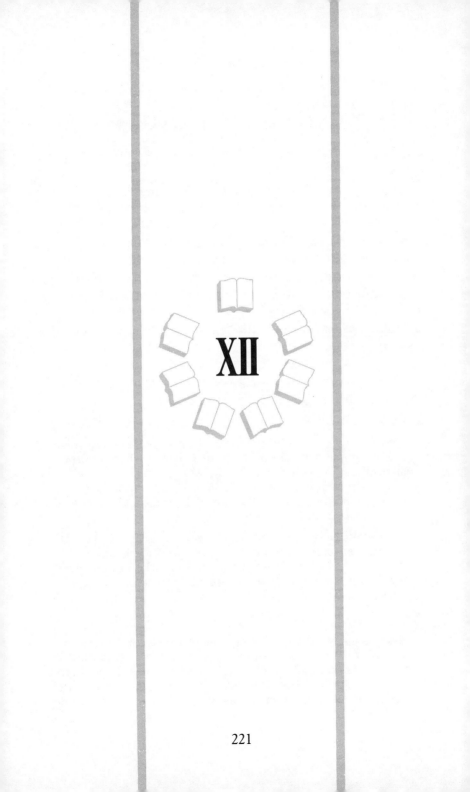

XII

By and About José Ortega y Gasset

(1883–1955)

José Ortega y Gasset, Spain's most famous twentieth-century philosopher, said: "I was born on a rotary press." His paternal grandfather founded *El Imparcial,* Madrid's leading newspaper; his father was its editor-in-chief and a regular contributor; and the Gassets, his mother's family, were also in publishing. Ortega himself started several newspapers and popular journals during his life and constantly wrote for them and other publications. Newspapers and journals were an appropriate outlet for a man who called himself a "philosopher in the marketplace."

Ortega's writings reflect his wide range of concerns and his belief that philosophic ideas have enormous consequences for everyone.

On the possibilities and challenges of life:

> To say that we live is the same as saying that we find ourselves in an atmosphere of definite possibilities. This atmosphere we generally call our "circumstances." All life means finding oneself in "circumstances" or in the world around us. For this is the fundamental meaning of the idea "world." The world is the sum-total of our vital possibilities.

> To live is to be continually deciding what we are going to be. Do you see the fabulous paradox that this holds? A being that consists not so much in what it is as in what it is going to be and, therefore, in that which is not yet. This essential abysmal paradox is our life. This is not my fault.

On civilization:

> Restrictions, standards, courtesy, indirect methods, justice, reason! Why were all these invented, why all these complications created? They are all summed up in the word civilization. . . . By means of all these there is an attempt to make possible the city, the community, common life. . . . Civilization is before all, the

will to live in common. A man is uncivilized, barbarian, in the degree in which he does not take others into account. Barbarism is the tendency to disassociation. Accordingly, all barbarous epochs have been times of human scattering, of the pullulation of tiny groups, separate from and hostile to one another.

On the need of goals:

An "unemployed" existence is a worse negation of life than death itself. Because to live means to have something definite to do—a mission to fulfill—and in the measure in which we avoid setting our life to something, we make it empty.

On the need of concepts:

He who gives us an idea increases our life and expands reality around us. The Platonic notion that we do not look with our eyes but through or by means of our eyes is literally true: we observe by means of concepts. *Idea* in Plato meant point of view.

On specialization:

Previously, men could be divided simply into the learned and the ignorant, those more or less the one, and those more or less the other. But your specialist cannot be brought in under either of these two categories. He is not learned, for he is formally ignorant of all that does not enter into his specialty; but neither is he ignorant, because he is "a scientist," and "knows" very well his own tiny portion of the universe. We shall have to say that he is a learned ignoramus, which is a very serious matter, as it implies that he is a person who is ignorant, not in the fashion of the ignorant man, but with all the petulance of one who is learned in his own special line.

Students participate in a deception when they choose a course of study, according to Ortega y Gasset. They begin to study not because they feel a genuine need for some particular knowledge, but because they must study something. Ortega says that knowledge exists only for those who have need of it, and particular disciplines arise because people have felt a need for knowledge so badly they could not live without it. A student who studies a subject but does not feel this need is forced to pretend. Studying becomes something false and contradictory. Nonetheless, we must study, and in our selection Ortega struggles to resolve this dilemma.

On Studying

José Ortega y Gasset

We are going to study metaphysics, and in what we are going to do there is, for the moment, an element of falseness. At first sight, this idea is stupefying; but the stupor produced by the phrase does not take from it the dose of truth that is in it. In that phrase—note it well—we do not say that metaphysics may be false; this characteristic is attributed not to metaphysics, but to the fact that we are setting out to study it. We are not discussing a false element in any of our thoughts, but a false quality in one of the things that we are doing—the studying of a discipline. Because what I am saying, eminently valid for metaphysics, is valid for more than that; according to this, studying, in general, would be deception. . . .

I did not say that studying would be only a deception and nothing else; it may have facets, sides, ingredients that may not be false. But for me, the fact that some of the facets, sides, or essential ingredients of studying are false is enough to give my statement its own truth.

---

*A selection from *Some Lessons in Metaphysics*.

This last seems to me beyond dispute. For one simple reason. The disciplines—whether they be metaphysics or geometry—exist. They are here because men created them by brute force, and if they used that force, it was because they needed those disciplines so badly that they had to have them.

The truths that these disciplines might contain were found in the first place by one man, and were then rethought or rediscovered by others who added their own efforts to that of the first man. But if they found these truths, it is because they sought them, and if they sought them, it is because men had need of them, because for one reason or another they could not do without them.

And if they had not found them, those men would have considered their lives to be ruined. If, on the other hand, they found what they sought, it is evident that what they found was adequate to the need they felt. This, which is a commonplace, is nevertheless very important. We say that we have discovered a truth when we have found a certain thought that satisfies an intellectual need which we have previously felt. If we do not feel in need of that thought, it will not be a truth for us. Truth, for the moment, is what quiets an anxiety in our intelligence. Without this anxiety there is no place for this quieting. Similarly, we say that we have found the key when we have found a precise object which makes it possible for us to open a closet that we need to open. The exact search is soothed by the precise finding; the latter is the function of the former.

If we make the expression general, we will find that a truth does not properly exist except for the one who has need of it, that a science is not such except for one who seeks it eagerly, in short, that metaphysics is not metaphysics except for those who need it.

For one who does not need it, who does not seek it, metaphysics is a series of words or, if you like, a series of ideas which, although they are each thought to have been understood, definitely lack meaning; in order truly to understand something, and most of all metaphysics, it is not necessary to have what is called talent or to possess great prior wisdom. On the other hand, what is essential is a condition that is elementary but fundamental; what is necessary is to have need of metaphysics.

But there are various forms of wanting, of need to the point of beggary. If someone forces me inexorably to do something, I will necessarily do it. Yet this need to do is not mine; it did not surge up in me, but was imposed on me from the outside. For example, I feel the need of walking and this need arises within me—which is not to say that it is a whim, or a matter of taste. No. Besides being a need, it has about it something of an imposition in that it does not originate in my free will but is imposed on me from within my being; I feel it, in effect, as a necessity of *my own*. But when, on my going out to walk, the traffic officer makes me follow a certain route, I find myself with another need, one which is not mine, but comes to me imposed from the outside, and the only thing that I can do about it is to convince myself of its advantages by reflecting on them and, in view of them, to accept them. But to accept a necessity, to recognize it, is not to feel it, not to feel it immediately as a need of my own; rather, it is a necessity of things which comes to me from them, an alien need and strange to me. We will call this the mediate necessity, as contrasted with the immediate, which I feel as a necessity born within me, having its roots in me, indigenous, autochthonous, authentic. . . .

Well, now, when man sees himself obliged to accept an external and mediate need, he finds himself in an equivocal, ambivalent situation, because this is the same as being invited to make his own (which means to accept) a necessity which is not his. Whether he likes it or not, he must behave *as though* it were his; he is thus invited to share in a fiction, a falsehood, a deception. And although this man may put forth all his good will in order to feel *as if* it were his, this does not mean that he achieves this, nor is it even probable that he can.

Having made this clear, let us turn our attention to the normal situation of the man who is called on to study, if we use this word as meaning the studying that a student does; or, what is the same thing, let us ask ourselves what a student is. And the fact is that we then find ourselves with something as startling as was the scandalous phrase with which I began this course. We find ourselves faced with the fact that the student is a human being, male or female, on whom life imposes the need to study sciences for which he has felt no immediate, genuine need. Leaving aside the cases that are exceptional, we recognize that in the best of cases the student feels a sincere, if somewhat vague, need to study 'something'—in general terms, to know, to be instructed. But the vagueness of this wish testifies to its slender stock of authenticity. It is evident that such a state of mind has never led to the creation of any real knowledge, because such knowledge is always concrete, a matter of the precise knowing of this or that; and, according to the law (at which I have barely hinted) of the functional relationship between seeking and finding, need and satisfaction, those who created knowledge felt no vague desire for knowing, but a most concrete and specific desire to find out this or that specific thing.

This shows that even in the best of cases—and again, I repeat, saving exceptions—the desire to know, which the good student may feel, is completely heterogeneous and perhaps even antagonistic to the state of mind which led to the creation of a particular order of knowledge. Thus, the attitude of the student toward science is the opposite of that which stirred its creator. As a matter of fact, science does not exist in advance of its creator. He did not first find it and then feel the need to possess it; he first felt a need that was vital rather than scientific, and this led him to seek the satisfaction of that need. In finding this in certain ideas, the result was that these were the science.

The student, on the other hand, finds himself with the science already made, as with a mountain range that rises in front of him and cuts off his vital road. In the best of cases, I repeat, the mountain range of science pleases him, attracts him, seems good to him, promises him victories in life. But none of this has anything to do with the genuine need which led originally to the creation of this science. The proof of this lies in the fact that the general desire to know is incapable of becoming concrete in the sense of a strict desire for knowledge in a specific field. Apart, I repeat, from the fact that it is not desire which leads to knowledge, but necessity. The desire does not exist unless the thing desired existed earlier, in reality or at least in imagination. That which does not even exist at all cannot provoke desire. Our desires are fired by contact with what is already here. On the other hand, a genuine need can exist without there having to pre-exist—even in imagination— the thing which might satisfy it. One needs precisely what one does not have, what is lacking, what is not existent, and the need, the demand, is that much stronger the less one has, the less there is of what is required.

In order to see this clearly, we need not depart from our theme. It is enough to compare the approach of a man who is going to study an already-existing science with the approach of a man who feels a real, sincere, and genuine need for it. The former will tend not to question the content of the science nor to criticize it; on the contrary, he will tend to comfort himself by thinking that the content of the science which already exists has a defined value, is pure truth. What he seeks is simply to assimilate it as it already is. On the other hand, the man who is needful of a science, he who feels the profound necessity of truth, will approach this bit of ready-made knowledge with caution, full of suspicion and prejudice, submitting it to criticism, even assuming in advance that what the book says is not true. In short, for the very reason that he needs, with such deep anguish, to know, he will think that this knowledge does not exist, and he will manage to unmake what is presented as already made. It is men like this who are constantly correcting, renewing, recreating science.

But that is not, in the normal sense of the term, what the student's studying means. If the science were not already there, the good student would not feel the need of it, which means that he would not be a student. Therefore, the matter is an external need which is imposed upon him. To put a man in the position of a student is to oblige him to undertake something false, to pretend that he feels a need which he does not feel.

But there are objections that will be made to this. It will, for example, be said that there are students who deeply feel the need to solve certain problems that are involved in this science or that. Certainly there are people like that, but it is hardly sound to call them students. It is not only unsound, it is unjust. Because these are the exceptional cases of creatures who, even if there were neither studies nor science, would, by themselves, invent them for better or for worse, and would by the force of an inexorable vocation, dedicate their strength to investigating them. But . . . the others? The immense and normal majority? It is they, and not those other more venturesome ones, who bring into being the true meaning—not the utopian meaning—of the words 'student' and 'to study'. It is unjust not to recognize them as the real students, and unjust not to question with respect to them the problem of what studying as a form and type of human occupation is. . . .

The other objection one would have to make comes from remembering that boys and girls do feel a sincere curiosity and have their own enthusiastic preferences. The student is not a student in general, but one who studies science or letters; and this assumes a predisposition of mind, a hunger which is less vague and not imposed from the outside. . . .

This word 'curiosity', like so many other words, has a double meaning, one primary and of substance, the other pejorative and abusive, like the word "aficionado" which means both one who truly loves something, and also one who is merely an *amateur*. The true meaning of the word 'curiosity' stems from a Latin root, . . . the word *cura,* meaning the cared for, the *cares,* what I call preoccupation. From *cura* comes *curiosity.* Hence, in daily speech, a curious man is a careful man, a man who does what he has to do with attention, extreme care, and precision, a man who neither slights nor neglects whatever occupies him, but, on the contrary, is preoccupied with his occupations. . . .

If, for example, I search for the keys, it is because I am preoccupied with them, and if I am preoccupied with them, it is because I need them in order to do something, to occupy myself.

When this preoccupation is exercised mechanically, without sincerity or a sufficient motive, and it degenerates into a mere appetite, we have a human vice that consists in pretending care for what, in fact, we do not care about, in a false concern with things that are not truly going to occupy us, and, therefore, in becoming incapable of genuine preoccupation. And that is what the expressions 'curiosity', 'being curious', and 'being a curious one' mean when used in their pejorative sense.

So when it is said that curiosity leads us to this science or that, we may either be talking about that sincere preoccupation with science which I earlier called 'immediate and inborn need' (this, we recognize, is not usually felt by the student) or we refer to the frivolously curious, to the appetite for putting one's nose into everything; this, I think, could hardly serve to make a man a scientist.

These objections are, for the moment, inane. Let us not go further with idealizations of the harsh reality, with cherished ideas that induce us to weaken, to soften, to blur the edges of the problems; let us not put balls on the bull's horns. The fact is that the typical student is one who does not feel the direct need of a science, nor any real concern with it, and who yet sees himself forced to busy himself with it. This indicates the general deception which surrounds studying. But then comes the stiffening of that deception, almost perverse in its effect, for it does not lead the student to study in general, but to study broken into sectors leading to careers, with each career made up of individual disciplines, of this science or that. And who is going to pretend that a lad, at a certain year of his life, is going to feel the effective need of a science which his predecessors were moved to invent out of their own necessities?

Thus, out of so genuine and lively a need that men—the creators of science—dedicated their entire lives to it, is made a dead need and a false activity. Let us not spin illusions; in that state of mind, human attempts at learning cannot reach the stage of human knowing. To study, then, is something fundamentally false and contradictory. The student is a falsification of the man. Because man *is* properly no more than he genuinely is, out of his own intimate and inexorable necessity. To be a man is to be, to do only what he irremediably is. And there are an infinite number of ways of being a man, and all of them are equally genuine. One can be a man of science, or a business man, or a political man, or a religious man, because all these ... are constitutional and immediate needs of the human condition. But man by himself would never be a student, just as man by himself would never be a taxpayer. He *must* pay taxes, he *has* to study, but he *is* by nature neither a taxpayer nor a student. To be a student or to be a taxpayer is an artificial state in which man finds himself by obligation.

This, which may have sounded so stupefying when we first pronounced it, becomes the essential tragedy of the teaching profession, and in my judgment, the reform of education ought to begin with that brutal paradox.

Because the activity itself—the activity which pedagogy regulates and which we call studying—is humanly false, something happens that is not as much emphasized as it should be; namely, that in no order of life is the element of falsity so constant, so habitual, and so tolerated as it is in teaching. I know full well that justice also may be false, and that abuses are committed in the courts. But weigh the comparision for yourselves, out of your own experience, and tell me if we would not be quite content if there did not exist within the teaching activity any greater inadequacy and abuse than are suffered in the juridical order? What is considered in the courts as intolerable abuse—that justice not be done—is in teaching almost the norm: the student does not study, and if he does, putting his best will into it, he does not learn; and it is clear that if the student, for whatever reason, does not learn, the professor cannot say that he is teaching; at the very best, he is trying to teach but is not succeeding.

Meanwhile, generation after generation, the frightening mass of human knowledge which the student must assimilate piles up. And in proportion, as knowledge grows, is enriched, and becomes specialized, the student will move farther and farther away from feeling any immediate and genuine need for it. Each time, there will be less congruence between the sad human activity which is studying, and the admirable human occupation which is true knowing. And so the terrible gap which began at least a century ago continues to grow, the gap between living culture, genuine knowledge, and the ordinary man. Since culture or knowledge has no other reality than to respond to needs that are truly felt and to satisfy them in one way or another, while the way of transmitting knowledge is to study, which is not to feel those needs, what we have is that culture or knowledge hangs in mid-air and has no roots of sincerity in the average man who finds himself forced to swallow it whole. That is to say, there is introduced into the human mind a foreign body, a set of dead ideas that could not be assimilated.

This culture, which does not have any root structure in man, a culture which does not spring from him spontaneously, lacks any native and indigenous values; this is something imposed, extrinsic, strange, foreign, and unintelligible; in short, it is unreal. Underneath this culture—received but not truly assimilated—man will remain intact as he was; that is to say, he will remain uncultured, a barbarian. When the process of knowing was shorter, more elemental, and more organic, it came closer to being felt by the common man who then assimilated it, recreated it, and revitalized it within himself. This explains the colossal paradox of these decades—that an enormous progress in terms of culture should have produced a man of the type we now have, a man indisputably more barbarous than was the man of a hundred years ago; and that this acculturation, this accumulation of culture, should produce—paradoxically but automatically—humanity's return to barbarism.

You will understand that the problem is not solved by saying, "All right, but if studying is a falsifying of man, and if, in addition, it leads, or can lead, to such consequences, let us not study." To say this would not be to solve the problem, but simply to ignore it. To study and to be a student was always, and is now above all, one of man's inexorable needs. Whether he wants to or not, he has to assimilate the accumulation of knowledge under pain of succumbing, either as an individual or as a group. If a whole generation should cease to study, nine-tenths of the human race then alive would die a violent death. The number of men now living can continue to subsist only by virtue of the superior techniques of making good use of the planet that the sciences make possible. Techniques can be taught, mechanically. But techniques live on knowing, and if this cannot be taught, an hour will come in which the techniques too will succumb.

So one must study. This, I repeat, is one of man's needs, but it is an external, mediate necessity like moving to the right as the traffic officer directs when I need to go walking. But between the two external necessities—studying and moving to the right—there is an essential difference which is the thing that converts study into a substantive problem. In order for traffic to function perfectly, it is not necessary that I feel an intimate need to go to the right; it is enough that I do, in fact, move in that direction, that I accept the need for this, that I pretend to feel it. But it is not the same with study; in order for me truly to understand a science, it is not enough for me to pretend the need for it within myself; or, what is the same thing, it is not enough that I have the will to accept it; in short, it is not enough that I study. It is also necessary that I should genuinely feel the need of this, that I be spontaneously and truly preoccupied with its questions; only then will I understand the answers it gives or tries to give. No one can thoroughly understand an answer unless he has understood the question to which it replies.

In this way, the case of studying is different from that of walking to the right. In the latter, to achieve the anticipated effect, it is sufficient that I do it well. In the former, this is not so; to succeed in assimilating a science, it is not enough for me to be a good student. Therefore, we have in this something man does which contradicts itself; it is at once both necessary and useless. Man must do it in order to achieve a certain end, but the result is that he fails to succeed. Because both things—its necessity and its lack of utility—are equally true, studying is a problem. A problem is always a contradiction which intelligence finds facing it, a contradiction which pulls it in two opposite directions and threatens to tear it apart.

The solution to so crude a two-horned problem may be inferred from what I have said; it does not consist of decreeing that one not study, but of a deep reform of that human activity called studying and, hence, of the student's being. In order to achieve this, one must turn teaching completely around and say that primarily and fundamentally teaching is only the teaching of a need for the science and *not* the teaching of the science itself, whose need the student does not feel.

Perhaps some of you have been asking yourselves, "What has all this to do with a course in metaphysics?" . . . Let us give a clearer justification of having begun this way, anticipating a first definition of metaphysics, the one that looks to be most modest, the one that no one will dare invalidate. Let us say that metaphysics is something that man does, something man makes—at least some men; later, we will see whether or not all men do it, even though they might not be aware of it. But this definition is not sufficient, for man does many things, and not merely metaphysics; indeed, man is an incessant, inescapable, pure doer. He makes his house, he makes politics, he makes industry, he makes verses, he makes science, he creates patience, and at the very moment that he seems to be doing nothing, he is in fact waiting, hoping, and your experience will confirm the fact that waiting and hoping is a terrible and most anguished process. . . . And he who neither waits nor hopes, . . . he who truly does nothing, makes that nothing; that is to say, he sustains and supports the nothing which lies within himself, that terrible, vital emptiness which we call boredom, spleen, desperation. He who does not hope despairs—a form of activity that is so horrible, requiring so wild a force, that it is one of those which man can least exhaust; he usually carries it to the extreme of making an actual and absolute nothing, of destroying himself, of committing suicide.

Among such varied and omnigenous activities, how can we recognize the one that is certainly metaphysical? For this, we will have to put forth a second and more precise definition: man engages in metaphysics when he seeks a basic orientation in his situation.

But what is man's situation? He finds himself not in one, but in many different situations; for example, you find yourselves in one now. You happen to be in the situation of setting out to study metaphysics; two hours ago, you found yourselves in another situation, and tomorrow you will be in still another. Now, all these situations, however different they may be, coincide in being parts of your lives. Man's life seems to be made up of situations, just as matter is composed of atoms. As long as one lives, one is living in a specific situation. But it is evident that just as all these situations, however different they may be, are vital, so there will be in them an elemental, basic structure which makes all of them situations within the realm of man. That generic structure will be made up of what they have in essence of human life. Or to put it another way, whatever may be the varied and variable ingredients which form the situation in which I find myself, it is evident that that situation will be me living. Therefore, man's primary situation is life, is living.

And we say that metaphysics consists of the fact that man seeks a basic orientation in his situation. But this assumes that

man's situation—that is, his life—consists of a basic disorientation. This is not a matter of man's finding himself, in his own
life, partly disoriented in this or that respect—in his business,
or in his strolling through the countryside, or in politics. He
who is disoriented in the country looks at a map or a compass,
or questions a passerby, and this is enough to put him right.
But our definition presupposes a total and fundamental dislo-
cation; that is to say, it is not that man happens to be disoriented, to be losing himself in life, but that, insofar as one can see,
man's situation, his life, in itself *is* disorientation, is being lost,
and, therefore, metaphysics exists.

Interpretive Questions

1. Can studying be made into a legitimate pursuit, according to Ortega?

2. Why does Ortega define truth as that which quiets an anxiety in our intelligence?

3. Why does the need to know, but not the desire to know, lead to knowledge?

4. In assimilating a science, why is it not enough to be a good student?

5. What is the difference between teaching a subject and teaching the *need* of a subject?